A FIELD GUIDE FOR
IMMERSION WRITING

* * *

A Field Guide for Immersion Writing

MEMOIR, JOURNALISM,

AND TRAVEL

* * *

Robin Hemley

THE UNIVERSITY OF GEORGIA PRESS

ATHENS AND LONDON

a
Friends Fund
publication

Publication of this work was made possible, in part, by a generous gift
from the University of Georgia Press Friends Fund.
Published by the University of Georgia Press
Athens, Georgia 30602
www.ugapress.org
Designed by April Leidig
Set in Arno Pro by Graphic Composition, Inc.
Printed digitally in the United States of America

Library of Congress Cataloging-in-Publication Data
Hemley, Robin.
A field guide for immersion writing : memoir, journalism,
and travel / by Robin Hemley.
p. cm.
Includes bibliographical references.
ISBN-13: 978-0-8203-3850-7 (hardcover : alk. paper)
ISBN-10: 0-8203-3850-8 (hardcover : alk. paper)
ISBN-13: 978-0-8203-4255-9 (pbk. : alk. paper)
ISBN-10: 0-8203-4255-6 (pbk. : alk. paper)
1. Reportage literature—Authorship. 2. Creative nonfiction. I. Title.
PN3377.5.R45H46 2012   808—dc23   2011044424

British Library Cataloging-in-Publication Data available

Excerpts from *Paper Lion* by George Plimpton reprinted by the permission of
Russell & Volkening as agents for the author. Copyright © 1966 by George Plimpton,
renewed in 1994 by George Plimpton.

For Jennifer Koski
and my other former students
who have let me be a part
of their writing lives.

Contents

Acknowledgments

I'm grateful to the following for their wise counsel and their enthusiasm for this volume. Erika Stevens initially approached me to write this book. I'm grateful to her for her enthusiasm for the idea and for nudging me to write it. I'm also grateful to Regan Huff, to whom the baton was passed; Regan was equally enthusiastic and helped me through the editing process. Likewise, I'd like to thank Dorine Jennette for her good catches, sharp insights, and enthusiasm for the book. I'd also like to thank Nicole Mitchell at The University of Georgia Press, my colleague Bonnie Sunstein for her support and recommendations, my former classmate from the Iowa Writers' Workshop, Eileen Pollack, for her expertise, Hattie Fletcher at the magazine *Creative Nonfiction* for her witty insights into the form, and Kate Lee at International Creative Management. I'm grateful to the Virginia Center for the Creative Arts for giving me the space and time I needed to kick-start this project. Finally, I'd like to express my gratitude to those busy writers who took time out of their schedules to answer the questions I put to them about their own experiences with immersion writing: Bob Cowser, Martin Goodman, Stephanie Elizondo Griest, Melissa Pritchard, Joe Mackall, and Dale Maharidge.

A FIELD GUIDE FOR
IMMERSION WRITING

* * *

An Introduction to Immersion Writing

Its Similarities and Differences from the
Traditional Memoir and Traditional Journalism

In Defense of the Vertical Pronoun

Every few months I read or hear of a fresh attack on the memoir. Very little excuse is needed to trigger the righteous indignation of a reviewer in the *New York Times* or another media outlet. A bad night's sleep. Indigestion, perhaps. In 2009 a *New York Times* reviewer for the *Sunday Book Review*, Judith Shulevitz, observed that "the attack on memoir [is] now a regular editorial exercise [and] dates back to the advent of journalism itself" (November 20, 2009). Two years later, Neil Genzlinger launched his own editorial exercise of the type to which Shulevitz referred, a humorously bilious attack on the genre in which he pined for "a time when you had to earn the right to draft a memoir, by accomplishing something noteworthy or having an extremely unusual experience or being such a brilliant writer that you could turn relatively ordinary occurrences into a snapshot of a broader historical moment" (*New York Times*, January 28, 2011).

Of course, Genzlinger covers his bases by including the criterion of "brilliance." That pretty much gives a get-out-of-oversharing-free card to any writer he designates "brilliant." Being of a similarly wistful bent, I might indulge in longing for a time when all journalists, fiction writers, and poets were of equal measure to Edward R. Murrow, Kafka, Borges, and Lorca. And I might likewise long for a time when newspapers such as the *New York Times*, instead of publishing screeds against memoir, weren't ruled by the same market forces that give rise to sensational memoirs, and reviewed books by poets or gave at least as much space to fiction as nonfiction. And let's not forget those halcyon days when journalists didn't share their opinions. Ah, the Good Old Days.

It's not hard to take potshots at memoir. Start by saying the word. Stretch it into a kind of English drawing room parody of pronunciation. *Mem-wah! I'm off to write my Mem-wahs!* But a lot of the hair-trigger enmity for the memoir that engenders such "regular editorial exercises" as Genzlinger's seems to me akin to that old vaudeville routine, "Slowly I Turned," in which an otherwise reasonable and mild-mannered guy goes completely bonkers in a kind of posttraumatic meltdown every time his unwitting companion says the word *Cincinnati*. As soon as the dreaded word is uttered, the mild-mannered guy's face turns demonic and he chants in a kind of insane drawl, "Slowly I turned, step by step, inch by inch . . ." completely lunatic to the point that he doesn't even know that he's thrashing the poor guy beside him, who is wholly innocent and ignorant of the reasons he's being attacked. Memoir Dread (known more scientifically as "Genzlinger's Affliction") often seems triggered by something just as private and eccentric as in the comedy routine. What else would account for the disdain of an entire form of writing?

Not ANOTHER gummy wad of autobiographical drivel! We can't stand it. Hang us from our thumbs, but don't subject us once again to your medi-ocre traumas, your whiny regrets, your tawdry victimizations. You are not the most important person on the planet! ("*I am!*" we might imagine such Grand Memoir Inquisitors intoning, or at least thinking privately.) *We're tired of the Self. Of Painful Lives.* (Ostensibly, this is the waggish name of a section of one London bookstore: the Painful Lives section).

Genzlinger goes so far as to suggest that ordinary people living ordinary lives should simply shut up and let the pros do their jobs. I should add that when I was in graduate school writing fiction, I shared Genzlinger's suspicion of ordinary people. Who wants to read about ordinariness? A well-known movie at the time, called *Ordinary People,* revealed (drum roll, please) that ordinary people have feelings and se-crets and tragedies, too. Who would have thought?! Betraying a cul-tural certainty that this could not truly be the case, one of the present-ers, in reading the nominees for best picture that year at the Oscars, renamed the film *Ordinary Movie*. Ordinary or not, this film from 1980 took away four Oscars, including Best Picture, Best Director (Robert Redford), Best Actor (Timothy Hutton) and Best Adapted Screenplay

(Alvin Sargent). And no wonder. The most persistent and sacred of lies is that any family is perfect, and families go to great lengths to preserve this myth. That's essentially what this film was about—in an affluent family, one of the sons dies in an accident and the family, especially the parents, pretends it never happened. But the son, Timothy Hutton, completely messed up as a result of his family's dysfunction (the term was not common parlance back then) sees a psychiatrist, Judd Hirsch, who heals Timothy Hutton by urging him to speak the truth, thus allowing him to win an Oscar. Okay, not quite as simple as that. Perhaps an old bout of Genzlinger's Affliction is flaring up in me.

As it turns out, a lot of people not only wanted to watch a movie about the large tragedies of small lives, but to read about them, too. And oddly, not as fiction. Memoirs by ordinary people have been with us for a long time. But in my parents' day, they used to be known as "first novels." In the past, what we might now call a memoir was typically the writer's first work of fiction, the kind known as a *roman a clef* (this, too, preferably said in a British accent), or a thinly veiled autobiographical novel. It used to be great literary sport to read a novel and try to figure out who the writer was *really* writing about.

To me, the film *Ordinary People* marks a watershed in our cultural fascination with and fear of telling our dirty little secrets. I'm not claiming that the film was responsible for the steady climb in memoirs written by ordinary people, starting around that time, but rather that the film tapped into a cultural shift that's both positive and negative in its literary ramifications. Around this time, I started noticing an unsophisticated suspicion of anything not labeled as "fact": "I only read true stories," a stranger told me more than once, betraying a certain literal-mindedness in the American psyche that's frightening. This suspicion of anything that isn't "factual" is its literary manifestation. In a way we have become a nation of literary fundamentalists—many people only care about something if they think it really truly happened. Many only watch TV if it really happened. American fiction for many years had been moving steadily toward realism, entrenching it within the academy as the only proper form of fiction. But once ordinary people started writing memoir, the idea of realism jumped the tracks. Why read fiction when nonfiction did realism better?

This seems akin to what happened to the painting world in the nine-teenth century when photography was introduced. As soon as one could point a machine at a table and create a reproducable image that was far more accurate than a painting, the need for paintings to rep-resent the empirical world mostly vanished, and what resulted was a greater move toward abstraction in painting, though of course photog-raphy didn't restrict itself to the literal image for long, either.

When I was the editor of *The Bellingham Review*, a literary magazine, I received an autobiographical essay by a then-unknown writer named Meghan Daum. The essay, titled "Variations on Grief," at a glance seemed to be the same kind of exercise in oversharing that Genzlinger laments in his *Times* piece. I'm sure I even felt a shudder of dread as I began to read Daum's essay. That dread must have left me in a flash because the sensibility at play made this unlike any other grief essay I'd ever read. At the heart of the essay was not so much grief as guilt, and a kind of determination that Daum professed, to not waste her life. Her friend Brian, the subject of the essay, had been in life a spoiled and apparently vapid man who had dropped dead in his early twenties of a mysterious illness, perhaps hantavirus—and yes, his death alarmed Daum and her friends, but it also seemed oddly justified to them. Here's how she characterized her feelings:

> When he left this planet, he left me and very few others, and if those Christian alternatives to life really exist, then he must know by now that we will never be reunited. If those opposable H's are true, then he is in Heaven for never committing any crime, and I'll find myself in Hell one day for the spin that I have put on his death. My spin is this: I believe that he couldn't do anything other than die. None of us who grew up with him could imagine an alternative. And the fact that he didn't of-ficially kill himself was enough to make all of us believe in the super-natural, or at least some kind of devilish warden hovering over our lives, whispering in our waxy ears, "Do something, or die." (159)

I'd like to say that Meghan Daum's voice is honest here, but is it that? It might be better to say that it seems "authentic." Authenticity is nearly as slippery a term as "honesty" when it comes to capturing experience on the page, but note that I wrote that the voice *seems* authentic. It works in the reader's mind to convince him or her that what s/he's getting is The Real Deal, the author herself, the inner workings of her mind. And yes, you are, in a sense, but nothing can truly capture the workings of a human mind in all its complexity. It *seems* authentic is as far as I'm willing to venture.

Still, authenticity, in its myriad forms, is one of the things we strive for as writers, in the form of a compelling voice that seems honest. We're concerned with language here, not simply the slopping down of words. The passage I've quoted, for all the seeming authenticity of its commentary on matters of life and death, is highly modulated and controlled. Even the phrase "opposable H's" feels original, confident, and clever.

Yet the *New York Times* review that appeared after the publication of this essay in Meghan Daum's debut collection, *My Misspent Youth*, used the occasion of a positive review of Daum's book to slam the genre in general. The reviewer, Louise Jarvis, opened with a shot across every memoirist's bow: "Meghan Daum is not an eccentric exhibitionist or a self-indulgent memoirist" (April 8, 2001). I'm sure Daum was glad to read that about herself. But Daum seems as eccentric to me as they come, and reveals herself to be as much of an exhibitionist as any writer when we read the modicum of self-loathing in these words toward the end of the essay, referring to a mutual friend who visited Brian's parents:

> Like a good person, he sat in the living room and spoke honestly about this horrible thing that had happened. Unlike me, he saw no reason to lie. Unlike me, he wasn't hung up on some twisted symbolism, on some mean-spirited rationalization employed to keep fear at bay, to keep grief a thing depicted in movies rather than a loss felt in one's own flesh. (174–75)

Remember, I published this. I don't really think it's self-indulgent. I'd like to say it's honest, brutally so, but really, how would I know? Instead, I'd rather state that it seems to me authentic in that it shows a version of someone else who deeply resembles a version of myself that I'd rather keep hidden. In *that* way it's self-indulgent. It indulges a Self, but not only Daum's. Mine as well. And most likely yours. Yet, if we use the typical standards by which we bash the memoir, I think we'd have to say that Meghan Daum ticks off at least a couple of those dreaded boxes:

Ordinary person? Yes.

Eccentric exhibitionist? Afraid so.

Self-indulgent? Not really, though I can imagine someone thinking her so. She's self-revealing, and that's often wrongly equated with being self-absorbed or self-indulgent.

It's not the subject that matters. It's the execution. Above all, Daum's use of language is precise and original, and this trumps everything. In this important way, she's by no means ordinary.

Of course there are different ways to write about or include the Self in your writing other than memoir, and this book will discuss and examine and yes, advocate for these ways in detail. Travel writers were once attacked with the same regularity as memoirists are today. From the late eighteenth century until the end of the Napoleonic Wars, travel was curtailed for most Europeans, and it wasn't until the upheavals ended that travelers resumed the traditional circuit of Europe known as the Grand Tour. Prior to this time, Grand Tours were largely embarked upon and written about by young male aristocrats, but the 1820s and onward saw a democratization of travel, and a large number of ordinary people writing accounts of their travels for publication. Behind this democratization followed the critics who wished the ordinary people would just shut up and let their betters write the travel books. One reviewer (though, oddly, *not* a *New York Times* reviewer) complained, "It is certainly somewhat extraordinary that of the great number of travelers sent forth by the peace from this country, with the design of recording their adventures, so few should have deviated from the most frequent routes" (quoted by Betty Hagglund in "The 'Bricolage' of travel writing: a Bakhtinian reading of nineteenth-century women's writings about Italy," paper presented at "Travel Writing: Practice, Pedagogy, and Theory," Asia Research Institute, National University of Singapore, February 24, 2011).

I'm not wholly unsympathetic to such criticisms. Deviation from the most frequent routes seems to me to be a fair request to make of the travel writer, the memoirist, and even the journalist. What drew this nineteenth century critic's ire, as well as Genzlinger's, and not unfairly, is that too often writers and publishers alike rely on *not* deviating from the most frequent routes. It's the faddishness of the enterprise that's worrisome—that a book might be published because it fits a prede-termined type of book that has little value other than its familiarity to readers who want more of the same. But this is no more true of the writings of ordinary people than of the writings of the great and accom-plished. How many of those people who have accomplished something "noteworthy or [had] an extremely unusual experience" actually write the memoirs with their famous names on them? Not many, I'd venture. The celebrity ghost-written book is at least as common as the Misery Memoir. Having led an interesting life should no more earn you the right to pen your *mem-wah* as having led an outwardly boring one if the writing itself lacks vigor and originality.

It's never the ordinariness of the person we should condemn, but the ordinariness of the writing, of the vision itself. Now, no one disputes the right of an ordinary person to write a travel book. We do not require that only aristocrats write travel memoirs (though of course travel itself is still the privilege of the relatively well-to-do).

Old-school journalists were taught to eschew that pesky *I* in favor of a more "objective" voice. But as most of us know in this postmodern age, there's no such thing as objectivity. Everyone has a unique perspec-tive, and even if you think you're being objective when you report, say, from a war zone, you have blind spots. There are things you ignore, you forget, or you don't notice due to your own cultural baggage and belief systems. In anthropology, it's known as *confirmation bias*, the tendency to notice those things that confirm your beliefs and ignore those that don't, and everyone is susceptible to it.

Of course, not all journalists express hostility toward the first person—or what I once heard waggishly referred to as "the vertical pronoun"—or even memoirs. Nearly every journalist I've met has a memoir in his or her drawer. While journalists are traditionally told to avoid the first person, I have met many a journalist who feels confined and oppressed by the inability to acknowledge the existence of the self while writing.

I sometimes think that attacks on the memoir aren't simply masking an upset stomach, a bad night's sleep, or an acute case of snobbery, but are instead the death bellows of the wounded old-school journalist, who still valiantly waves the banner of Objectivity while lies, biases, and opinions catch him in the gut and bring him to his knees. *You bloody memoirists! My death will not go unavenged!*

Not only is the self worth investigating and including on the page, but it is perhaps the only way to approach those slippery terms of *honesty* and *authenticity*. To write about the world without putting on the table your biases, your psychological indigestion and unhealthy sleep patterns, is in a sense to falsify—a kind of falsification not so bald as the memoirist's who lies about his supposed war exploits, but disingenuous in its own fashion.

Forms of Immersion

Now that I've launched what I hope is a spirited defense of the memoir, I propose to leave the traditionally reflective memoir behind for the rest of this book. It's the groundwork for this book, but not the book itself. I'm more concerned here with other types of writing that employ the self, but which aren't exclusively *about* the self. I'm interested here in books that actively engage the world around the writer via what's known as *immersion writing*.

Immersion writing engages the writer in the here and now in a journalistic sense, shaping and creating a story happening in the present while unabashedly lugging along all that baggage that makes up the writer's personality: his or her memories, culture, and opinions.

Immersion writing has existed in various forms for centuries, but hasn't been called that. I'm using the term loosely as a catch-all that includes any kind of memoir, travel narrative, or journalistic piece in which the narrative is as much forward-looking as backward, and in which the writer is a part of the story being told.

The three types of immersion writing that we'll examine here are immersion journalism, travel writing, and what I call the immersion memoir. Each form engages and utilizes the self but for different purposes. In the immersion memoir, the writer writes about the world in order to examine the self. In immersion journalism, the writer includes the self in order to write about the world. With travel writing, it's a bit of both, the travel writer writing about herself in the world and in a sense the world in herself. In each case, the writer is not making claims of objectivity, but sees his or her subjectivity as a kind of advantage. The *I* becomes a stand-in for the reader, an anchoring consciousness who develops a rapport with the reader and in effect stakes claims of reliability and authenticity: this is what I saw. This is what I did and observed. Trust me that I'm being as accurate as possible, but draw your own conclusions.

Within each of these three forms of immersion writing, I've designated subcategories, what we might think of as organizing principles. One of the most difficult aspects of writing anything is finding its form, and so I've tried to help you shape and organize your writing by suggesting possibilities and supplying examples that other writers have employed previously. I offer one caveat, and I'm only going to state this once, so please pay attention:

These organizing principles are not hermetically sealed. A piece of writing can easily fit more than one category. The aim here isn't to make you into a good categorizer. The categories are meant to be useful, not binding.

Chapter by chapter, I discuss how each of the various forms of immersion writing (immersion journalism, immersion memoir, and travel writing) can be considered in five ways: as quest, experiment, investigation, reenactment, or infiltration. While I employ these five subcategories, I don't write about them in the same sequence in the various chapters. I'm not trying to create some kind of airtight scientific taxonomy. I want to mix it up a bit. And the subcategories are not equally important to each of these forms. For example, the quest is a common form within travel writing, but not quite so common in immersion journalism. The experiment is common in immersion memoir, but not as common in travel writing. I don't list these subcategories strictly in order of importance within each chapter, but order of importance is my guiding principle.

If your goal is an outward exploration of the world, then you're most likely an immersion journalist. If your goal is to explore yourself, if you don't mind being called an oddball (as I don't!) then you're more of a memoirist, as interested in your own transformation as the rest of the world's. But I'd argue there's overlap. There always is. The point is that the self matters, and it's unrealistic—perhaps disingenuous—to believe it doesn't. It's not the only thing that matters, of course, but when I read a work of nonfiction, I have questions. More often than not, I want to know who's telling the story and why. I want to know what's at stake for the writer. That doesn't necessarily mean I need to know everything about the writer—it's a matter of degree and intent and the nature of the project.

Chapter One

Immersion Memoir

The first question we have to ask is this: aren't all memoirs immersions? Isn't that one of the criticisms of them? The answer is simple. I don't mean immersion in the sense of yet deeper self-involvement. On the contrary, the immersion memoirist takes on some outward task or journey in order to put his/her life in perspective. As I mentioned in the introduction, the difference between immersion journalism and immersion memoir is that an immersion journalist is primarily interested in reporting on the world outside herself while using the self as the vehicle for that information. The opposite is true of the immersion memoir. The immersion memoirist is interested in self-revelation or evaluation while using the outside world as his/her vehicle.

The immersion memoirist is interested primarily in understanding the Self, that tricky and elusive notion, and not so small a task. As Emerson wrote, "To believe your own thought, to believe what is true for you in your private heart is true for all men—that is genius. Speak your latent conviction, and it shall be the universal sense" ("Self-Reliance"). To write honestly about the Self more often takes courage and generosity than egoism.

When I was an undergraduate in college, I majored for a while in anthropology. At that time, many anthropologists still pretended they were dispassionate observers of other cultures—at least the idea of relativism hadn't quite trickled down to my classroom yet. The case of early ethnographer Frank Cushing was handed to me and my classmates as a cautionary tale, an example of an ethnographer losing his objectivity and "going native," for which he was roundly criticized in his own time, the Victorian era.

What made Cushing so unusual was that he not only lived with and observed the Zuni tribe of New Mexico for five years, but he *became* a Zuni, integrating so well into their culture that he learned the language, the customs, was adopted by the pueblo, and was even initiated into the priesthood. From a contemporary view, at least from my point of view, his experiences were nothing short of amazing. What a privilege, what an extraordinary insider's view. But imagine what strength of character this man must have had to seek such experiences at a time when when Native American cultures were largely derided as "savage," misunderstood, and at best exoticized. Widely dismissed by the anthropological establishment until at the least the late 1980's as an "oddball," as one text refers to him, it's hard now to find a single criticism of his participatory style of ethnography, which is considered "ground breaking" and "ahead of its time." Certainly, Cushing was not the first to live with a tribe, but he was the first to live so intimately with a culture different from his own in a way that valued their customs and beliefs as much as his own, if not more so, and to communicate his insights to a wider audience. Perhaps one reason the establishment considered him such an oddball was that he was so public about his appreciation of the Zuni culture. He became something of a celebrity when in 1882, his accounts of living among the Zuni were featured in three of the most fashionable magazines of the time: *The Atlantic Monthly, Harper's,* and *Century Illustrated Monthly Magazine,* as well as *Popular Science.* Illustrations showed a ritually scarred Frank Cushing dressed in Zuni ceremonial garb being inducted into the Priesthood of the Bow, and his accounts of life with the Zuni were anything but academic or weighted with the pretense of objectivity. In fact, his accounts in *My Adventures in Zuni* are loaded with charm as he describes his sense of culture shock when he first made the decision to live among the Zuni, thinking his white traveling companions would leave him with sufficient provisions for two months. To his dismay, they left him with nothing. When one of Cushing's Zuni hosts notices his sadness at his friends' departure, he asks why his "little brother" is sad.

> "Alas," I replied. "My friends are all gone, and they have left me nothing."
>
> He looked at me a moment and said, "Little Brother, you may be a Washington man, but it seems you are very poor. Now, if you do as we tell you and will only make up your mind to be a Zuni, you shall be rich, for you shall have fathers and mothers, sisters and brothers, and the best food in the world. But if you do not do as we tell you, you will be very, very, very poor indeed."
>
> "Why should I not be a Zuni?" I replied in despair; and the old man quickly answered, "Why not?"
>
> Leaving me for a few minutes, he soon returned with a steaming bowl of boiled mutton, followed by his kindly old wife, bearing a tray of corncakes mixed with chili and sliced beef, which, wrapped in husks, had been boiled like meat dumplings.
>
> "There, try that," said the old man, as he placed the bowl in the center of the floor. "Fill your stomach, and your face will brighten."
>
> And the old woman stood admiringly by as I heartily ate my first genuine Zuni meal. (43)

Here clearly is a story, the beginning of a great adventure. No wonder he was excoriated by academics. He didn't wash all the personality out of his prose in an attempt to appear objective. He knew how to tell a story. He wasn't afraid of being a part of the story he wanted to tell. While certainly the book was as much about the Zuni as himself, at the center of it was his personal transformation, and that in part is what made it so engrossing to audiences of the time and so anathema to academics, who perhaps considered themselves above transformation, at least in print.

Without a doubt, the book that was most enjoyable for me to write and most satisfying in many regards was my own immersion memoir, *Do-Over! In Which a Forty-eight-year-old Father of Three Returns to Kindergarten, Summer Camp, the Prom, and Other Embarrassments.* I've also written traditional journalism and a traditional memoir, but the confluence of these forms in the immersion memoir allowed me to satisfy both aspects of my personality, the pensive soul with a reflective bent, and the equally strong part of me that loves to travel, to meet people, to experience the world. For me, the immersion memoir combines the best that traditional memoir has to offer with the best of journalism. While immersion memoirs certainly have their critics, they also have plenty of fans.

I had the idea for *Do-Over* when I was sitting around with some of my graduate students and we were chatting about impossible things we'd like to do.

"I'd like to go back to summer camp, but as an adult," I said. "I was never a very good athlete when I was a kid, but now I bet I could beat a bunch of campers at basketball and soccer and capture the flag."

My students loved the idea and urged me to propose it to a magazine. I did so and the first editor to whom I suggested the piece liked the idea and even admitted that it seemed like something his magazine might go for, but nonetheless, they weren't going to sign on. The fact that one magazine rejects your idea for any reason or no reason is discouraging, but should never make you give up. Another magazine might think the idea is brilliant. In my case, the second editor I approached, Faye Penn of *New York Magazine*, loved the idea and passed it on to her boss, Adam Moss. Within an hour of my e-mail to her, I had a reply: "This is irresistible," she wrote, "but can you pull it off?"

A fair question, but I knew from experience that part of making anything work is to say, yes, I can make it work. In my proposal, I wrote that I'd either like to go to the oldest summer camp in America, with which I had no real connection, or to Camp Echo in the Catskills, where I had experienced a disastrous stint as a counselor when I was eighteen. Faye said that *New York Magazine* would only sign on to the project if I could convince Camp Echo to allow me to return to their camp for a week. So I called up Camp Echo and was eventually put through to Marla Coleman, the director of the camp. I told her I had once been a counselor there and what I proposed to do—a little like *Billy Madison*, I suggested, to give her the sense of the spirit of the project. It helped that

New York Magazine wanted to commission the piece. Marla seemed to have a sense of humor and liked the idea.

"Of course you'll have to undergo a background check like any counselor," she said, almost apologetically.

Of course! I told her I'd be surprised if they didn't want me to undergo a background check.

I was in. Just like that. Long ago, I learned to appreciate what the telephone can do for a writer. In my early twenties, I worked as a lowly mailing clerk at *Playboy Magazine* in Chicago. My friend Peter Nelson called me one day and asked me to help him out. He was working on a story about . . . urinals, and felt he needed someone to vouch for him with the company that made most of them in America. So I wrote a letter on *Playboy* letterhead to the president of the urinal company and told him that Peter Nelson was writing a piece on urinals that I thought would turn out great. I hoped that they would give him "every assistance with his research." Of course, the letter implied all sorts of things I had no right implying, though with a take-home pay of two hundred dollars a week, I wasn't terribly concerned. And I wasn't actually *saying* that *Playboy* was going to publish his piece on urinals. Okay, okay, it was dishonest. You've got me. But Peter took his tour and presumably wrote his story, though I never heard any more about it from him. I wouldn't recommend such a stunt, but the point is that writers sometimes need a little chutzpah to get a foot in the door.

Many years later, I recalled Peter's moxie and gained my own courage from it. I knew that the assignment was not going to be easy. Much of my summer had already been planned and I had only a small window within which to go back to summer camp, a week that overlapped the end of July and the beginning of August. As the story centered so much on summer, the editors at *New York Magazine* told me I'd only have a few days to write the story, because they'd want to get it into one of their August issues. They'd kill the article, otherwise.

A friend of mine and his partner have a lovely house on the Jersey shore and they offered to lend it to me for the two days I'd have to write the story before my deadline. The plan was that I'd write the story, turn it in, Faye Penn and Adam Moss would pronounce it brilliant, and I'd live happily ever after.

But here's a complication. It's one thing to have an experience, but it's quite another to get a handle on it, to understand from what angle you're going to approach the piece, and to have sufficient distance to have such perspective. When you're writing on deadline, you don't have a lot of time to muse.

And here's another complication. You can go into an experience wanting to write about it in one way, but then something else intrigues you or distracts you, or you're unable to see the experience clearly, and suddenly you're left with a prose blob rather than a crafted essay. *Prose blobs* (yes, that's the official name for them) sometimes read like a journal or diary or a sloppy blog post. At the end of the prose blob, the reader often turns the page and looks for missing pages. Is that all? Yes, that is all, unfortunately. Don't try looking for missing pages. There are none. Sadly, the last person to recognize a prose blob most often is its creator. The prose blob ultimately is about nothing and everything. That's why it's a blob.

In my case, I jammed a summer's worth of activities into five days of camp. I went horseback riding, took a swim test (which I barely passed), attended Luau Day, went mountain biking, played golf, dodgeball, basketball, cleaned up my bunk, ate loads of candy, wrote letters home, said the Pledge of Allegiance, swung on a trapeze, rode a zip line through the trees, sang camp songs, played catch, and ate awful camp chow.

I carried with me at all times a pocket-sized notebook, and I never experienced anything without cracking the notebook open and writing down everything and anything that caught my eye: dialogue, details of camp life, observations, brief character sketches. I knew that while it was a pain to constantly record what I saw and experienced, when I was writing the piece, my notes would be invaluable and make that end of the job much easier. You might wonder if carrying around such a notebook might make both myself and the people around me self-conscious. Certainly, it did, at first. But I liken it to a documentary film-maker or photographer who is constantly taking pictures of a subject.

At first, the subject feels stiff and self-conscious, but the longer the photographer sticks around, the more s/he becomes a part of the furniture, and the subject starts loosening up. That's certainly what I found. The notebook was also a bit of a shield for me, at first. I felt a little foolish going into the project, a forty-eight-year-old man bunking with a bunch of ten-year-olds, who, by the way, more or less accepted me and my project, and thought it was a fun idea. But at first the notebook allowed me to constantly remind myself and others that I wasn't just some creepy old guy wanting to relive his misspent youth, but *a professional writer with an agenda.* Happily, after a couple of hours, I didn't really need the notebook as a shield any longer. I relaxed and started to enjoy myself.

My intention had been to write about the differences between my childhood and childhood as kids experienced it now. I told the editors at *New York Magazine* that I had been a terrible camper, a poor physical specimen. That much was true. I told them that now I wanted to return to summer camp to beat all those ten-year-olds at dodgeball and basketball, using my thirty-eight-year advantage against them. That part was slightly exaggerated. In this regard, at least, I'm a little more mature than that, but in any depiction of yourself on the page, you're going to exaggerate some aspects of your personality while playing down others. The person you are in real life is not exactly the same person readers will meet on the page, though we like to pretend otherwise. It's a persona, a construction, and while you certainly don't want to pretend to be something you're not, a little exaggeration for comic effect and the like is standard operating procedure for the writer. You don't want to overdo, of course, or you risk presenting yourself as a caricature.

By the time I had completed my Herculean task of returning to summer camp, I felt exhausted and exhilarated, but I still had a three-thousand-word article to write. A note: when an editor tells you three thousand words, that's what she means. If you turn in a piece double the size, the piece might be killed—or worse, might be cut down to size using all the care and elegance of a document shredder.

So for two days, I holed myself up in my friends' house on the Jersey shore, writing all day, trying to distill my notes into something readable and purposeful. Confidently, I turned it in and flew off to a conference in Tacoma, Washington, where I was scheduled over the next several days to teach, give a reading, and give a lecture. A day later, I received a call from someone at *New York Magazine* and was told that I had created a prose blob, in so many words. When such a verdict is delivered, my first reaction is always a familiar sinking feeling, but what choice do you have but to buck up and find out what needs to be done to make the piece acceptable? There was a lot to do, apparently. A lot needed to be overhauled, and what had happened to the angle about me wanting to best the ten-year-olds at their games? I had completely dropped that angle from the piece.

I received the call in the morning and was told that I had until nine a.m. the next day to rewrite the piece entirely. Or . . . The alternative hung in a transcontinental silence. Nine a.m. East-Coast time. Six a.m. my time.

Oh, great, I thought. Easy. On this particular day, I was giving a lecture, conducting a workshop, and giving a reading that night. I did all three, trying to forestall the rising panic I felt. As soon as my reading was done, I sprinted out of the building and headed to a local supermarket, where I bought as much junk food as I could possibly stand. It reminded me of summer camp—"bunk junk," the campers called it.

And then I wrote. Somehow, in about three hours, the piece crystallized once I had the first lines down. For me, finding that first line, a line that captures precisely the tone you want the piece to take, makes the job so much easier. The newly revised piece began in this way:

> It's 9 p.m., and I'm in the cookies-and-milk line with 350 other campers. Or at least I think it's the cookies-and-milk line. If there's a line at Camp Echo, I get in it. Two campers, Blake and Randy, and their counselor, Mike, stand in line in front of me, and they're not moving to my satisfaction. "Line's moving slow, huh?" I say, glancing at my watch, but they just look at me. I guess type-A personalities don't belong in the cookies-and-milk line. Finally, I get my tiny carton and my oatmeal-raisin, and join my 10-year-old bunkmates from cabin B5-2. They're gathered on the deck of the "Nest," a fifties-style diner, what I would have called the Canteen back in my first go-round as a camper more than 40 years ago. (par. 1)

I don't recall how I began the original piece, but this was stronger. I began in the scene and also captured a certain attitude I wanted to have with such phrases as "type-A personalities." Happily, the editors were delighted by this version of the piece and it ran two weeks later with the title, "Big Man on Camp."

While ensconced in my little writing retreat on the Jersey Shore, I thought I could probably write an entire book of these "do-overs," and after the article was accepted, that's exactly what I told my agent. In about five minutes I was able to come up with a list of ten do-overs, embarrassments from my childhood that I wanted to have a second shot at. These included going back to the prom with a woman I'd had a crush on when I was sixteen, but was too shy to ask out, reprising my role as The Heavenly Messenger in *The Littlest Angel*, a play in which I flubbed a line when I was seven, going back to kindergarten, taking a standardized test, and joining a fraternity, among others.

The idea of wanting a second shot at life's regrets is pretty universal. I wrote a fairly brief proposal of about ten pages and included the *New York Magazine* piece, and within a couple of weeks, the book sold.

I'm not trying to brag, but rather to show the steps involved, that while this was a pretty heady moment in my writing career, it was also a kind of beware-what-you-wish-for moment. I still had to write the book, and to do so, I had to convince any number of people to allow me to do things that might strike them as odd or creepy. But I possessed the naive sense of optimism I carry into every book project, and naive optimism can give you a fair bit of momentum.

Early on, my editor and several others asked me some important questions and gave me some crucial cautions to consider. The most crucial of these is that there's a big difference between a magazine article and a book. A book, at least this type of book, needs some kind of narrative glue, or what's often referred to as a "through story." My publisher didn't want this book to be a series of magazine pieces, some loosely-themed essays that had no real glue.

What was the through story? they wanted to know, and . . .

What was at stake?

In other words, what was my motivation for writing the book? It couldn't be because, well, I like to see my name on a book jacket. In any memoir, and this is certainly true with the immersion memoir, there has to be something more substantial at stake emotionally for the writer. If there isn't, then yes, you're simply writing for the sake of the gimmick, and the reader will soon lose interest. We have to care about the protagonist of the story, and we can only do so if we see what's at stake, what your motivations are, and how your project compliments your life—or, more frequently, troubles it. "The key is that the topic has to be fascinating to me," says A. J. Jacobs in the article "Meet the Gimmick Books" (*Los Angeles Times*, September 5, 2009). "I have to have real passion. I am a writer and this is what I do, so it has to be interesting to readers. But it has to have stakes for me."

It wasn't that difficult to come up with the stakes in this book. I have three daughters, from two marriages, and in many ways, the book would be about this, about parenthood, fatherhood specifically. Like a lot of dads, I'm loving but certainly flawed, and in some ways I saw this as an opportunity to write a letter of sorts to my daughters, to see what was happening in their lives, and to record and muse upon what was going on in their lives while I tried to perform my do-overs.

So, essentially, there were two stories here: the story of my do-overs and the story-behind-the-story, the story of my daughters. I think there should always be two stories in a sense. You should always ask yourself, "What is the story here?" and then, "What's the real story?" Conceptualizing in such a way adds texture to your story, layers it, makes it seem more than simply a superficial treatment of your subject, a gimmick.

The Reenactment

My book *Do-Over* might be classified as a reenactment. Clearly, in many of my do-overs, I was working from an original event. I really did flub a line in my school's production of *The Littlest Angel* when I was seven, and I really did find a theater group in Marietta, Georgia, staging a production of it, and they were kind enough to let me reprise my role. There's something undeniably powerful about reenactment—some people spend every waking minute thinking about the past and trying to make it come alive again, trying to inhabit their own past, or more often, an original event that they were not a part of to begin with. Think of Civil War reenactors. Why do they do it? I'm not sure because it's not my obsession, and there are probably dozens of reasons why people would want to put on period costumes and shoot cannons at one another. The Romanian philosopher Mircea Eliade speculates that people in their sacred rituals are nearly universal in their attempt to return to a kind of "golden age" that the ritual replicates. Think of the Eucharist in Christianity, or the myth of the murdered and reborn Egyptian god Osiris. There's even a fellow in the Philippines who has himself crucified—not fully crucified, of course, which would be a one-off—but he's actually nailed to a giant cross and hangs there for a while. Not the kind of reenactment I heartily endorse, and I have to say that I wouldn't want to read this guy's memoir, even if there is something obviously at stake (no pun intended).

One of the most well-known reenactments of recent years is Julie Powell's *Julie and Julia: 365 Days, 524 Recipes, 1 Tiny Apartment Kitchen*. This project started as a blog, became a book, and then a movie. Essentially, it's a reenactment of Julia Child's introduction to the American palate of haute cuisine, Julie Powell's attempt to cook all of Julia Child's recipes in *Mastering the Art of French Cooking, Vol. 1*. Of course, it wasn't a complete reenactment, because that would have been boring and useless. Why do the same thing over in exactly the same way, and with the same goals in mind? That's unoriginal. No, the reenactor modifies the original and changes it to suit her own goals. In a way, the reenactment becomes a kind of vehicle or metaphor for the author to discuss other important issues in her life: in this case, Julie Powell's flagging marriage and self-esteem. Whether the effort was successful or not is up to you as a reader, but it's not surprising that Julia Child herself was not a fan of Julie Powell's project. Child died a year before the book appeared, but she had seen Powell's blog and dismissed her as someone who wasn't a serious cook. Fair enough, but I'd argue that Powell's book wasn't really about cooking, or not in the same way as Child's book. It was a book that used cooking as an organizing principle, as a metaphor to discuss other issues.

In *Trials of the Monkey, An Accidental Memoir*, by Matthew Chapman, the author, a successful (if largely unproduced) screenplay writer and director, and, more importantly for this story, the great-great-grandson of Charles Darwin, decides to ride the bus from New York City to Dayton, Tennessee, to cover the annual reenactment of the famous Scopes "Monkey Trial," held in 1925, at which the theories of Darwin were on trial. It's hard to imagine a better setup than this, but as I've said, there has to be something at stake for the writer for the book to have any weight at all, and Chapman sets about laying out his stakes right away. It's worth quoting here the entire brief prologue to illustrate how clearly and skillfully Chapman sets the tone of the book, tells us what's at stake, and then tells us what's *really at stake*, using a tactic commonly known as the *bait and switch*. Most good authors employ the bait and switch — it's a means of texturing a book, to give it the kind of depth that's needed in order to sustain any longer work; it's useful for most shorter works as well. A good book is almost always about more than one subject. And book projects are protean: you start out thinking you're writing about one thing, but the book you write almost never turns out to be the book you set out to write. Here's how Chapman states it:

> In the spring of 1998, Tom Hedley, publisher of Duckworth, invited me to write a book. He had read a screenplay of mine and felt I could handle something larger. I decided I'd like to write about the 1925 Scopes "Monkey" Trial, the trial of a schoolteacher convicted of teaching evolution in defiance of Tennessee law. This was not an arbitrary choice. My great-great-grandfather was Charles Darwin, something I had given little thought to as an adult until I came to America and discovered his theories were still rabidly contested. A recent poll found that 40% of those surveyed favoured teaching creationism instead of evolution in public schools. In 1999 the Kansas Board of Education voted to delete virtually every mention of evolution from the state's science curriculum.
>
> I suggested to Tom that I should take a Greyhound bus from New York, where I live, down to Dayton, Tennessee, the small town where the trial took place. Apart from doing historical research, I would also find out what had changed in the town in the past seventy-five years, if anything. I had heard that once a year the town staged a re-enactment

of the trial. I would cover the event, the largest in the town's calendar, and this would become the hub from which I'd throw out the other spokes of the intended work. We could even call the book *The Voyage of the Greyhound*.

What I hadn't taken into account was that I was on the verge of my own crisis, spiritual and otherwise. I'd been writing screenplays for ten years, two or three a year, each one overlapping the next, and had taken only one vacation during that time where my computer had not accompanied me. Some years I made close to a million dollars but I was never more than a month or two away from bankruptcy. I was married to a beautiful and interesting woman, had a stepson I liked and admired, and a daughter I adored; but when I left New York in June, I was in a rage at my excessive life and all the obligations and stresses of middle age.

And then I was on the bus. At first I thought about the trial, then about my own connection to it. By an accident of birth, I was the descendant of one of the most influential men of the last two millennia, a man whose research and theories challenged not only Christianity but most other religions as well. How much of my sense of failure and panic, I wondered, could be traced to my freakish antecedents?

Now, when I looked out the window, what came to mind were scenes from my past, waves of them, too many to ignore. In particular, I thought about my mother, great-granddaughter of Darwin, a woman of enormous promise and intelligence whose decline into alcoholism was one of the great puzzles of my childhood. I started writing some of these memories into a second notebook. Another book, a book within a book, began to form, an accidental memoir, fragments of an overshadowed childhood. I could have suppressed this, but I began to see that what initially seemed a diversion from my main purpose might in fact be entirely part of it. The fundamentalists who tried to banish the theory of evolution from the schools did so because they feared it would destroy faith in God and leave only a vacuum in its place, and here was I, up to now a more or less cheerful and defiant atheist, suddenly overwhelmed by an inexplicable sense of spiritual emptiness.

I had fallen off the rails. Perhaps this other book would help me climb back on. (ix–x)

Perfect. This prologue sets out the parameters of the book, not only letting the reader know what's at stake, but also providing a kind of map of the book, what to expect on this author's journey. The reenactment is simply a vehicle for the narrator's self-discovery. It's a story of psychological evolution, not mere reenactment we're embarking upon. We might even call it *The Voyage of the Ego*.

This notion of the prologue is worth touching on briefly. Three out of my four nonfiction books have prologues—a prologue isn't necessary or advisable for every book, but I think it's a good idea to write one. It's not only a way to let the reader know what you're writing about, but it's a good way for you to know what you're writing about. Even if you don't wind up using it, writing a prologue is a valuable exercise.

What Chapman engaged in was a historical reenactment, though the trials form only a small portion of the book—not only was he reenacting the trials, but he was reenacting his life, something that all memoirists do.

If you choose to write about a reenactment, you might cast about for some historical event, but of course it should have something to do with your life, your interests, your obsessions, your dreams. You don't have to be the great-great-grandson of Charles Darwin to cover the reenactments of the Scopes "Monkey Trial," but it helps. Otherwise, what's your connection? You're a human being? Okay, that's a start, but that doesn't really sell me on the idea.

Not too long ago, I went to a ceremony commemorating General MacArthur's raising of the American flag at the end of World War II on the battle-scarred island of Corregidor in the Philippines. (No one dressed like MacArthur in full military uniform with sunglasses and corncob pipe, but it was still a reenactment). I've spent a lot of time in the Philippines, and I've written about it before, and I was living there for a year with my wife and family. A friend of mine, Peter Parsons, whose father had been a war hero in the Philippines, asked me if I wanted to spend a few days on the island with some of his friends who all had connections to the war. Corregidor was an important American stronghold that fell to the Japanese several months after the bombing of Pearl Harbor on December 7, 1941. While the rest of southeast Asia fell rather quickly against the onslaught of the Japanese, the defenders of Corregidor held out without reinforcements for an incredible five months. MacArthur was whisked away in the dead of night before the island fell (very much against his wishes) so that he could help plan the Allied counteroffensive in the Pacific. You might remember that MacArthur famously said, "I shall return." Return he did in 1945, after a fierce and costly battle to regain the island. As the American flag was once again raised over the parade grounds of the island, he famously said, "I see that old flagpole still stands. Have your troops hoist the colors to its peak and let no enemy ever haul them down."

The other people attending this somber ceremony included the son of an American survivor of Corregidor and the Japanese prison camps, the curator of the MacArthur Memorial in Norfolk, Virginia, and other sons of veterans of the war in the Pacific. My only association with the island was my fascination with its haunted landscape, the bombed out buildings, the knowledge that thousands of men on both sides had died defending or assaulting it. I wrote in part to figure out why I wanted so much to be there:

> I'm not sure why I'm here except that I love Corregidor. I love digging around in history. But I'm not a full-throttle Corregidor buff. I probably wouldn't choose to live here and my father wasn't a war hero. Perhaps in that I'm fortunate. Less to live up to, in this regard at least. I am definitely the least relevant of this rag tag platoon. If this were a war movie, I'd be the fresh meat who lands on the island, lights a cigarette and gets his fool head blown off before he even opens his mouth. ("Dispatches from Manila: Old Ghosts of Corregidor," *McSweeney's Internet Tendency*, April 5, 2010)

We're always writing to find out what we think, not because we know something about the world and want to impart it to everyone else. At least, this is true in virtually any memoir. We've all been cornered at parties by people who want to tell us some bit of wisdom they've gleaned about the world. In my experience, they tend to be the biggest boors I'll ever meet. I'm much more of a questioner, and I like to be around people who question as well. I try to take that attitude into my writing. If you already know everything, you're not open to new knowledge. So, in a piece such as this, I'm always asking myself, why

is this important to me, why should I care? I found my answer toward
the end of the essay, when I saw that this was about my father and me,
both of us writers who sat out wars—well, I was fortunate in that I was
of military age in between wars (Vietnam and the first Gulf War). But
the very knowledge of this fortune haunted me in a way, too, at least as
long as I was on Corregidor. More importantly, my father's early death
has haunted me my entire life. And the war's legacy haunts me, too. To
whom and what do I owe my life? It's a big question:

> Really, we were all there for them, even me, though my father's biggest
> war accomplishment was writing the *History of Censorship in the Mid-*
> *Pacific* (a classic, I'm telling you!), for which he, Lieutenant Hemley, was
> given a special commendation from his superiors. I never really knew
> him because he died when I was only seven. But I have a desk job, too. I'm
> a writer like him, and I'm out here for him, reenacting and preserving the
> memory of all those poor guys who died on this island. It's boggling for
> me to think of all their unborn children, my Never playmates, my Never
> fellow reenactors. The world is crowded with the ghosts of their collec-
> tive possibility. As odd as this makes me feel, I probably owe my life to
> the atomic bomb. My father lobbied successfully finally to be shipped
> overseas and was on his way to be part of the invasion of Japan when the
> Bomb dropped. It's not hard to guess his fate: the Japanese would not
> have surrendered (of the roughly six thousand Japanese soldiers on Cor-
> regidor, fewer than fifty survived) and I would have been nothing but an
> asterisk in my father's dead eyes on some Japanese beach. ("Dispatches
> from Manila")

In essence, there are two types of reenactments, the personal and the
historical. But even when we're dealing with a historical reenactment,
as in Chapman's case and in mine, inevitably the historical and the personal merge.

The Experiment

The most popular form of immersion memoir to write can loosely be
termed *the experiment*. In each case, the author sets about a task, often

for the better part of a year, and in the course of that year, discovers the meaning of life, the secrets of the universe, or simply some tenet of existence that has heretofore eluded him or her. In *The Year of Living Biblically*, A. J. Jacobs gives himself the inspired and entertaining task of trying to live by the Bible's precepts, all of them, for a year. At once a sociological study and a personal discovery, the book's task presented itself because, Jacobs says, as a secular Jew, he didn't seem to have the spiritual needs of much of the rest of humanity, and wanted to see whether the rest of the world was deluded, or if he was missing an important element of being human. Of course, the notion of following everything in the Bible to the letter might be considered a little silly, if not absurd, but the absolutist nature of his quest brought about insights, personal and cultural, that he might not otherwise have discovered. Sure, it's laudable to try not to covet thy neighbor's wife, gossip, or tell falsehoods, but how does a rational and contemporary soul regard the notion of stoning adulterers, not shaving, or the admonition not to wear clothes of mixed fibers? The answer to these questions is charming, funny, and smart, but it would be nothing if Jacobs hadn't been willing to make the book ultimately about himself. In so doing, he had to write about his relationships with others and the tensions caused by his project, primarily with his wife.

On day two of his project, Jacobs finds that growing his beard out is about the least difficult of biblical laws, while the simple task of deciding on a night's entertainment with his wife is littered with all kinds of spiritual roadblocks.

I sit down at the kitchen table. Julie is flipping through the Arts and Leisure section of the *New York Times* trying to decide on a movie for Saturday night.

"Should we see *The Aristocrats*?" Julie asks.

Huh. *The Aristocrats* is the documentary about the dirtiest joke ever. It contains at least half a dozen sex acts specifically banned by the Book of Leviticus. Julie could not come up with a worse suggestion for an evening activity. Is she testing me? She's got to be.

"I don't think I can. It doesn't sound very biblical."

"You serious?"

I nod.

"Fine. We'll do something else."

"I don't know if I should be seeing movies at all. I have to think about that."

Julie lowers her gaze and looks at me over the top of her glasses.

"No movies? For a year?"

I'm going to have to choose my battles these next twelve months. I decide I'll bend on this one for now—I'll phase out movies slowly, giving Julie a little grace period.

Things, after all, are kind of tense in our house right now. Julie had a hard time getting pregnant with our first child . . . We did eventually succeed (we have a son named Jasper), but apparently, practice did not make perfect, because the second time around is just as much of an ordeal.

In the last year, I've been—as the Bible says—uncovering Julie's nakedness. A lot. Too much. Not that I dislike it, but enough is enough. You know? It gets tiring. Plus, Julie's getting increasingly frustrated with me because she thinks I'm micromanaging—always quizzing her about ovulation times and basal temperatures and her five-day forecast. (17–18)

To break it down, notice how Jacobs gives us a scene at the kitchen table followed by a summary of one of the main concerns of his life over the past few years (the couple's difficulty conceiving). We don't know Julie and we don't know Jacobs, but he addresses us with the familiarity of a friendly confidant, as though speaking to someone whom he can trust. In turn, we're more likely to trust him.

It's also worth noting how close to his immediate consciousness we are in this scene. It's as though we're right there with him, experiencing his discomfort in the moment. It's as simple as that pause, "Huh," when Julie asks him if he wants to see *The Aristocrats*. This is an example of what author John Gardner refers to, in *The Art of Fiction*, as "psychic distance," which is basically the gap, varying in size, between the reader's mind and the narrator's. Think of it as similar to close-ups versus wide-angle shots in films. Most often, you don't want to see an entire film in close-up, but there are times when the director wants you to crawl into the skin of the character, and that's when a tight close-up is used. In the same manner, the writer modulates psychic distance. That "Huh" says a lot without saying a lot. It certainly would have been a waste of words and not as immediate if Jacobs had pulled back at that moment:

> "Should we see the Aristocrats?" Julie asks.
> This simple question catches me quite by surprise. I sit there utterly flabbergasted.

No need to go any further with that. "Huh" says it all.

In a similar fashion, Danny Wallace doesn't mechanically go about his project in which he vows to say yes to everything that comes his way. Well, he starts out mechanically, but soon the stakes get higher when he meets a woman to whom the possibility of anything comes quite effortlessly.

> It was like the world was full of Yeses or something. But I want you to understand—what I think it's *important* you understand—is that I wasn't saying Yes because I was playing the Yes game. I'd all but forgotten about that. I wasn't saying yes to prove anything to myself anymore, or to Ian, or to anyone else. I was saying yes because I *wanted* to. I was saying yes because all of a sudden it was coming naturally. I was saying yes because when you're in love the world is full of possibilities, and when you're in love, you want to take every single one of them.
> And that's my roundabout, slightly awkward way of telling you that . . . yeah . . . I was . . . you know . . .
> In love and all that.

Notice in Wallace's case the direct address to the reader, again as though you and I were his confidants, even to the point of imitating a young man's awkward admission to a friend that he's fallen in love. Obviously, in the privacy of his own home at his writing desk, he was not in that moment of awkwardness anymore. The events had all passed and Wallace was slyly recreating that moment of awkwardness by writing about it as though it was happening to him at the very moment he was setting words down on the page. And in a way, perhaps it *was* this way for him because as we all know, remembered emotion can hit us with as much force as when we first experienced it. In any case, what's important is that the reader feel viscerally what the writer wants him to feel—in this case, the opening up of the possibility of love and its attendant complications to a formerly closed-off narrator. Wallace is doing what most good memoirists do, showing us a mind at work on the page, even if the consciousness he's showing us is in some ways a recreation of his thoughts when he first fell in love, and so is presenting to us something both honest and an artifice at the same time.

An experiment can easily become a gimmick book if there's nothing at stake, if you're simply entering into the project because no one has done it before. Most of these experiments happen over the course of a year, which makes sense. You have to have some end point for your experiment and a year is a natural cycle. A day, a week, and a month are too short, but the near-universal time frame of a year adds sometimes to the sense of a formula, a gimmick.

As I was finishing *Do-Over*, I had a little fun with the gimmick concept. I wrote and published a poem that satirizes the desire to write a gimmick book simply because you want to publish a book.

Rejected Book Ideas

For a year, I'll wear one sock inside out.
For a year, I'll eat only Bibb lettuce.
For a year, I'll pretend I'm invisible.
I'll speak with a fake French accent for a year. *The Year of Speaking with a Fake French Accent.*
I will pee sitting down for a month—*The Month of Peeing Sitting Down.*
I propose becoming a serial killer for a year. For each murder, I'll use a different instrument of death, starting with an imitation of Lizzie Borden's axe murder of her parents. My parents are dead already, but I'll substitute the parents of my editor or agent.

I will be a prostitute for a fortnight. I will lie down with as many men
    and women as possible during that time and I will tell their
    untold stories. The working title will be *The John Voice Project*.
I won't look for trouble, but if I find it, I'll be ready. I will call this
    book, *Ready for Anything!* or *Come What May!* Which do you
    prefer?
I will have my hair cut, one hair at a time, by a thousand hair stylists
    around the world.
    Naturally, we must call the book *From Hair to Eternity*. And each
    book sold will come with a souvenir hair.
I will travel around the world in a baby carriage. No one has yet done
    that.
Or none of these. I might just write a book by hand on moth wings.
    This will be my memoir. But you will need to bend close as I
    write or I will be lost to you forever.
(*Ninth Letter* 6, no. 1 [Spring/Summer 2009])

The Jazz Age was also the Age of Stunts, and people used to pass around
stunt scrapbooks in which they would commemorate various stunts,
such as flagpole sitting, dance marathons, and goldfish swallowing. The
completion of the stunt was its own object, and the scrapbook was as
literary as these things got, for the most part. There aren't a whole lot of
stakes in goldfish swallowing (except, obviously, for the fish), and so far
I haven't heard of a book titled, *Memoirs of a Goldfish Swallower*, though
actually, I kind of like the title.

Other experiments that have been turned into books include *The Year of Yes*, by Maria Dahvana Headley, a woman who said yes to every man who asked her out on a date for a year; *No Impact Man: The Adventures of a Guilty Liberal Who Attempts to Save the Planet and the Discoveries He Makes about Himself and Our Way of Life in the Process*, by Colin Beaven (the biggest problem with all of these books, including my book, as I see it, is these absurdly long subtitles! Resist the subtitle if you can. At least, keep it short); *A Year Without "Made in China": One Family's True Life Adventure in the Global Economy*, by Sara Bongiorni; *Give It Up! My Year of Learning to Live Better with Less*, by Mary Carlomagno; *The Year of Living Like Jesus: My Journey of Discovering What Jesus Would Really Do*, by Ed Dobson; *The Guinea Pig Diaries: My Life as an Experiment*, by A. J. Jacobs; *Animal, Vegetable, Miracle: A Year of Food Life*, by Barbara Kingsolver; *Not Buying It: My Year Without Shopping*, by Judith Levine; *Helping Me Help Myself: One Skeptic, Ten Self-Help Gurus, and a Year on the Brink of the Comfort Zone*, by Beth Lisik; *Plenty: Eating Locally on the 100-Mile Diet*, by Alisa Smith and J. B. MacKinnon; *The Urban Hermit*, by Sam MacDonald; *Eat This Book: A Year of Gorging and Glory on the Competitive Eating Circuit*, by Ryan Nerz; *Living Oprah: My One-Year Experiment to Walk the Walk of the Queen of Talk*, by Robyn Okrant; *Reading the OED: One Man, One Year, 21,730 Pages*, by Ammon Shea.

When all these ideas are summed up in this way, they *do* sound pretty gimmicky. No wonder some people refer to this kind of immersion writing as "schtick lit." But here's a thought. Novels when they're summed up often sound melodramatic. Poems can't be summed up. And a good memoir can sound sensational and schlocky in summary. It's all in the execution. I haven't read all of these books, and there are some that appeal to me more than others. Not every experiment book will appeal to you or anyone else, and you can see how one book influences another. Several years ago I read Michael Pollan's influential book, *The Omnivore's Dilemma: A Natural History of Four Meals*, itself a work of immersion writing, though more journalism than memoir, as he's not really attempting to learn about himself so much as learn about food production using himself as a conduit. Still, it's an experiment. He first dines on a meal from McDonald's (though unlike Morgan Spurlock, the director of *Super Size Me*, it seems all he can do to make himself stomach one Big Mac) and then traces its origins. He does the same with three other meals, including one he has hunted and gathered. Barbara Kingsolver, Alisa Smith, and J. B. MacKinnon have a similar interest in the subject, but take a more memoiristic approach. In Kingsolver's book, she traces her family's decision to move from Arizona back to a family farm in Virginia to grow their own food and eat only local produce beyond that. Smith and MacKinnon, on the other side of the continent, decide to eat only food grown within a hundred miles of their Vancouver, British Columbia, apartment. They're all similar ideas, but as I said, it's a matter of execution. Even comparing the first lines of all three books illustrates their different approaches.

A. "The year of eating locally began with one lovely meal and one ugly statistic."

B. "The story about good food begins in a quick-stop convenience market."

C. "Air-conditioned, odorless, illuminated by buzzing fluorescent tubes, the American supermarket doesn't present itself as having very much to do with nature."

Can you guess whose line is whose?

I find it interesting that none of these first lines have the vertical pronoun in them—why is that? Perhaps the authors of these books want to establish a tone that is personal, but not so personal as to seem irrelevant to the reader's life. We see the larger stakes immediately in all three: "eating locally," "good food," and "nature." You can probably guess right off that the third line is Pollan's, but you might be hard-pressed to distinguish in tone and content Kingsolver's line from Smith and MacKinnon's. Both lines set up the expectation of an experiment and a narrative in nearly the same fashion: "The year of eating locally began . . ." and "The story about good food begins . . ." To me, that says something really telling about the nature of the experiment book: it almost always relies on chronology. You're not likely going to begin an experiment book at the end. You have to go through the stages, the process, before you're going to reveal the results.

The two books came out within one week of one another. But whose book is better? I'll let you be the judge. Obviously, Kingsolver is the more well-known author, but that doesn't mean she's written a better book. Writers take on the same subjects all the time—mostly, it's just coincidence, or something in the air or the water, the zeitgeist, the hand of God, you name it. It's uncanny how often it happens, three books on silence, for instance, coming out at the same time, and reviewed together in the *New York Times*. You shouldn't necessarily reject an idea simply because it's been done before. In fact, that's sometimes an advantage, as we'll see when we discuss the reenactment. And if you have competition, suck it up and write the best book you can. Hopefully, your competition won't be Barbara Kingsolver. When I was writing my book *Invented Eden*, about an alleged hoax in the Philippines (we'll look at that a bit later), I found out halfway through the project that the well-known Filipino-American writer Jessica Hagedorn was working on a novel about the same subject. We regarded each other a little warily during the writing process, but after our books were complete, we wound up doing a couple of events together as our books came out within six months of each other's.

It's all in the execution. Ideas are out there for the taking.

The Infiltration

This form of immersion is at least as common as the experiment. By definition, an infiltration is an immersion experience. But there are two kinds of infiltrations, because there are two kinds of infiltrators: spies and insiders. There's a fine distinction between the two. The spy has infiltrated as an impostor, hoping to gather information, and to take it back to report to the rest of the world. The insider, on the other hand, doesn't hide her identity, and might even be sympathetic to the circle she's penetrated. The infiltration is a common form of immersion journalism, so we'll be looking at infiltration through the lens of the journalist, too. But for now, I'd like to focus on personal infiltrations, more along the lines of Frank Cushing's experience with the Zuni. Cushing was the ultimate insider.

Let Us Now Praise Famous Men, the classic book James Agee created with photographer Walker Evans, is as much an infiltration into the human spirit as anything else. On assignment for *Fortune Magazine*, Agee and Evans chronicled in the most unconventional and eccentric way the hard-bitten and dirt-poor lives of three tenant farm families in rural Alabama in 1936. Smack in the middle of the Depression, Agee quickly found himself saddened and disturbed by what he saw, and respectful of the people whose lives he had been sent to describe. I don't know of a more honest and beautiful account of an outsider's attempt to see the inside of someone else's life. Interestingly, Agee refers to himself in the beginning of the book (somewhat facetiously) as "a spy, traveling as a journalist" (xvi), but if so, he's more of a double agent, because he's certainly not serving the interests of his bosses at Fortune Magazine or the U.S. Government. His sympathies are fully with the poor people he's come to infiltrate—he makes this clear at the outset when he quotes the famous communist rallying cry, "Workers of the world unite and fight. You have nothing to lose but your chains and a world to win" (xiii). Lest you immediately brand him a communist (whatever that means to you), he adds a footnote cautioning the reader not to pigeonhole him. He states, "[N]either these words or the authors are the property of any political party, faith, or faction" (xiii). And the book is no manifesto, but a lyric, a kind of love song to these families and the place in which they live. Throughout, the book is moving, the narrator open to the point of being wounded and vulnerable. Agee was only twenty-seven when he took the assignment, and his senses of idealism and anger are those of someone vital and unbent by life.

In one lovely scene, he writes of eighteen-year-old Emma, who married a man much older than her when she was sixteen because she didn't like her stepmother. Two years later, she's regretting it deeply. The man she married is terribly jealous and locks her at home when he goes to town and hardly allows her out of the house. When she runs away to her family home, he runs after her and begs her to return, which she does. Finally, he goes to Mississippi and buys a farm. He sends for her; a friend of his will drive her and their furniture from Alabama to Mississippi, far from all the people she loves and the only home she knows. Agee feels deeply sympathetic to her (and, truth be told, attracted to her, as does Walker Evans), and doesn't think she should go, doesn't want her to go, but feels helpless, as does the rest of her family, as does Emma herself, who seems powerless to make the choice she obviously wants to make. Agee writes:

> What's the use trying to say what I felt. It took her a long time to say what she wanted so much to say, and it was hard for her, but there she stood looking straight into my eyes, and I straight into hers, longer than

you'd think it would be possible to stand it. I would have done anything in the world for her (that is always characteristic, I guess, of the seizure of the strongest love you can feel: pity, and the wish to die for a person, because there isn't anything you can do for them that is at all measurable to your love), and all I could do, the very most, for this girl who was so soon going out of my existence into so hopeless a one of hers, the very most I could do was not to show all I cared for her and for what she was saying, and not to even try to do, or to indicate the good I wished I might do her and was so utterly helpless to do. (58)

Agee in some ways is a forerunner of the gonzo journalists of the 1960s, though much more earnest in his tone that Hunter S. Thompson or Tom Wolfe, whose portrayals of the 1960s druggie subculture dripped with irony. But I'd argue that much gonzo journalism fits more readily into the category of immersion memoir than immersion journalism, as its focus is squarely on the individual reporting the story.

Certainly, Hunter S. Thompson was a classic infiltrator, sometimes as insider, sometimes as a spy and provocateur. In 1970, in the very first piece of gonzo journalism, the piece for which the term was coined, Thompson infiltrated the Kentucky Derby in an essay saturated in his trademark fashion with booze, pranks, and blackouts. The piece is titled, "The Kentucky Derby is Decadent and Depraved"—which, by the way, the Kentucky Derby proudly displays on its Web site, proving Thompson's thesis, I guess! It's a brilliant lampoon, long on schtick and short on earnestness or actual information of any relevance, but no one writes a train wreck better than Thompson. Accompanied by British illustrator Ralph Steadman, Thompson pretends to be a *Playboy* photographer, drives a mammoth rental car (beer in one hand), and maces the head waiter at a restaurant. Along the way, he scares his English companion with dire warnings and anecdotes of the atavistic moneyed breed that annually attends the Derby. Is it all true? I very much doubt it. Who cares? I don't.

Do we learn about the Kentucky Derby? Not much. You can call it *gonzo journalism* all you want—the name has stuck. But it's not. It's twisted, hilarious immersion memoir, with Hunter Thompson as the ultimate insider. Louisville is where he was born and the Derby itself he sees as a besotted festival of inbred idiots, the emphasis on boozing, the horses the least interesting thing there. He keeps searching throughout the essay for the kind of alcohol-soaked bloated wretch he considers emblematic of the Derby, but seeing himself in the mirror at the end of the piece, he recognizes that he is the best representation of that sort he's yet come across.

Sometimes, a series of events we could never have anticipated or even dreamed of leads us from the role of observer to that of participant to complete insider, changing the course of our lives, if not our writing. Such was the case with the novelist and short-story writer Melissa Pritchard, a professor at Arizona State University, who in middle age found herself foundering a bit. Her parents had both died and her daughters had grown up and moved away from home to start their own lives. Quite by chance, she happened upon some articles about women soldiers deployed in Afghanistan, and by her own admission, she was so naive about the war, she hadn't even known that women were serving in Afghanistan. The articles, about women in the Air Force doing humanitarian work in the provinces, astonished her. The women, working in some of the most dangerous areas of Afghanistan, served on Provincial Reconstruction Teams (PRTs) in remote villages, delivering medical supplies, food, and education. Their value was immeasurable in that they could talk to Afghan women, while men couldn't because of traditional Afghan strictures.

"I guess I got seized," Pritchard told me. "I was moved by these women doing peaceful work. Something went off in me and I thought, 'I have to meet them.'"

Pritchard is a well-respected fiction writer, but she had virtually no press credentials or associations. A friend in the military put her in touch with someone in media relations, whom she told she wanted to pitch the article to *O Magazine*. She did eventually pitch the piece to them, but they wrote back politely and told her they had something similar in the works (an excuse that many magazines use, by the way). For their part, the military welcomed a positive story, but they weren't going to send a civilian to a dangerous area simply because she was curious. To date, she'd only written one journalistic piece, a feature for a local magazine on Sudanese refugees. She ricocheted around the military for three months in an arduous process of trying to secure the necessary permissions to go to Afghanistan, securing letters of support from any magazine that would help her. Eventually, a couple of magazines wrote her letters of support, and she presented these to one of her gatekeepers, a Sergeant Tynes at Baghram Air Force Base, who told her politely that he had never heard of these journals. But she was persistent, and they wrote back and forth every day until finally, he said, "Okay, you're good to go." But she wasn't. She still had reams of paperwork to fill out, and the military could still back out if the fighting heated up and they thought it too dangerous. And she still had to buy her own body armor. About a thousand dollars worth, from a place on the Internet. The box arrived two weeks before Christmas, the size of a double-wide refrigerator.

She went to Walgreens and bought a little red notebook and a tape recorder (which she never used). She was winging it. While she may have been a cub reporter, she was no stranger to placing herself in situations many would find dangerous, squalid, or distasteful. She had assisted on a medical mission to Ecuador, and before heading to Kabul, she flew to India, where she participated in a poetry project for children who live in the brothels of Calcutta. Her family knew about these adventures, but she told neither of her daughters that she was headed to Afghanistan.

Sitting in full body armor at Baghram Air Force Base, being briefed with soldiers before a mission on improvised explosive devices (IEDs) and what to do if she were captured by the Taliban, she thought, not so much afraid as somewhat stunned, "Oh my God, I'm in a war zone" (*O, The Oprah Magazine*, May 2010). All her months of preparation, and now she was here and it was real.

She went on missions with the soldiers and she took copious notes. Before this, she hadn't realized how observant she was, but she took notes wherever she went, and the soldiers wanted to talk, and she listened and wrote down what they had to say. She focused her attention on five women, but one in particular stood out, twenty-one-year-old Senior Airman Ashton Goodman. Pritchard writes of her:

I found that beneath her veneer of military protocol and discipline, beneath her bravado, kill-talk, and cussing, she was surprisingly vulnerable, coltish. She was also ravenous for adventure. As we drove from one
PRT mission to the next in this harsh, mountainous province, visiting
medical clinics, a fledgling radio station, a girls' school, an international
aid drop, I learned she was earning a degree in biology, planned to be a
veterinarian, was an amateur photographer and an aspiring author, writing 'little stories,' she said, to relieve stress. She had just started Rosetta
Stone Spanish lessons and confessed to missing bubble baths. She had
a tattoo on her left forearm, *Studium Nunquam Intereo*—"spirit never
dies. (*O, The Oprah Magazine*, May 2010)

After a couple of weeks, Pritchard flew back to Arizona to begin teaching the new semester, but found it difficult to adapt—she had seen
no violence, but still she felt it hard to adjust to her cozy and safe life.
She felt thoroughly muddled, and in this state she began to write and
research. First, she decided to tell the story by combining the ideas
of beauty and war. Then she started reading about the history of Afghanistan, then the poetry of Afghanistan, then the history of women
in Afghanistan. She initially wrote a fifty-page article that started with
the first woman's poem in Afghanistan. There was something fever-
ish about all of this writing, a complete absorption in the culture she
thought she needed in order to understand . . . what? Then she wrote
about burkas and the history of burkas and a group of Afghan women
known as the Burka Rock Band. She was at sea. Then someone suggested she might be writing a book, and she thought, *Oh no!* A word
to the wise: just because you're confused and don't have a handle on
your material doesn't necessarily mean you're working on a book. You
might be, but you might not. Mostly, it means you don't know yet what
you're writing about or why, and you need to discover what these things
are before the writing gels. Sometimes a piece of writing becomes a
prose blob because a writer keeps adding layer upon layer of complexity, when in fact the simplest approach to the piece might ultimately be
the best and most powerful.

Pritchard sent her fifty-page prose blob (an official term, remember!) to *Harper's*, and an editor she knew there told her she should really narrow it down, basically politely turning it down.

At this time, she started writing profiles of the five women she had traveled with in Afghanistan. She had returned from Afghanistan in January, and now it was May, and she still didn't have a handle on what she wanted to say.

The day she finished writing her profile piece, she logged in to her Facebook account and saw a funeral notice for Ashton. Thinking it must be some horrible joke, she visited Ashton's Facebook page and saw tributes and condolences to the young soldier who, she learned, had been killed near Baghram by an IED.

That summer, Melissa was scheduled to teach in a writing program in Prague for a couple of weeks. A few nights before her departure, she received some letters from Ashton's boyfriend, who was also stationed in Afghanistan. He was suicidal. "He was a stranger but we had Ashton in common. I remember lying in bed thinking I need to write about Ashton, but I was so tired of it all. There was only the germ of an idea" (conversation with author, August 14, 2010).

I was also teaching in that summer program in Prague, and I heard Melissa give a lecture about her trip and the profiles of the women soldiers, including Ashton. Her talk was moving and I asked to see what she'd written—she showed me the profiles—all well written, of course, but somehow they lacked the focus, and, more importantly, the passion with which she spoke about her experience. I approached her and asked if she'd like to have lunch with me and talk about her project, and she seemed eager to do so. The next day, we took the tram to a market I'd discovered and ate hotdogs at a picnic table while she told me about Ashton, and about Ashton's boyfriend—she told me how his best friend had also been killed, and how he had hoped to marry Ashton when they returned to the States. When he was at his lowest, cutting himself with a knife and thinking about suicide, a cat jumped into his lap. Ashton had loved cats and he was sure this was her, returned to comfort him.

I was mesmerized by her honest and emotional telling of the story in a way that I hadn't been by the more removed and distant voice of the profiles.

"You know what you have to do?" I said. "You have to write this story about Ashton. That's the story."

I should say that I felt reticent giving her this advice. She's an accomplished writer, but I sensed her uncertainty about writing nonfiction. I went so far as to outline possible ways to open the essay, though as you can probably tell, she's not someone who likes or needs to be told what to do. But she listened and I convinced her over that lunch that she needed to write Ashton's story and that she was able. The most important things I gave her were permission (because that's sometimes all we need, and it's something we don't always give ourselves), and my enthusiasm. Of course, she didn't take all my advice, nor did she need to. It was just a matter of someone sitting across from her and saying, "You know the story. Now write it."

Sometimes I wish I had someone to tell me the same kind of thing. It's a great and rare pleasure when someone feels as enthusiastic about your work as they do about their own.

She went home and wrote it. And when she sent it to me, I read it, and by the end tears were running down my face. And I'm not a sentimental or particularly weepy person. I wasn't the only one. When she sent it to her agent, her agent wept, and her agent's associates wept. Melissa unwittingly unleashed a fit of weeping around magazine offices all over Manhattan. Among other magazines, her agent sent it to O. After the editors at O finished weeping, they bought the piece—and remember, they were the first magazine she had approached, by whom she'd originally been turned down. The finished piece appeared in O in their 2010 tenth-anniversary issue, a year and a half after she returned from Afghanistan in a daze and a fog.

But the magazine article didn't give her peace or closure. There was one more thing she needed to do. With the help of others, she set up the Ashton Goodman Fund as part of the Afghan Women's Writing Project, and now, thanks to Melissa, there's an Ashton Goodman grant that raises money for Afghan women's education.

Let's reflect a moment on this—think about where Melissa Pritchard started in her understanding of the role of American servicewomen in Afghanistan: zero, nada, bupkes. There's no way she could have anticipated the outcome when she began. All she knew was that she needed to go to Afghanistan and "talk to these women." She was "seized." And remember, there were many moments of confusion before she knew how to write the story and what she wanted to say. The result is a lovely piece of immersion memoir, a unique work of infiltration.

Melissa Pritchard went from outsider to insider, not in a journalistic way, but as a memoirist does. While some of the information she imparts to the reader has journalistic merit, she becomes in her piece "Finding Ashton" more of an emotional insider.

I should add that I don't want to present myself in a self-aggrandizing way as Dr. Memoir, who amazes with his Laser-like Ability to Peer into the Hearts of Wayward Memoirists and His Uncanny Powers of Perception! Not at all, but it's almost always easier to see more clearly into someone else's projects than one's own. Often, it's just a matter of asking the right questions. Brainstorming is a significant part of my creative process in the writing of nonfiction—I love to brainstorm with others about their projects, and there are times when bouncing my ideas off someone else can make all the difference. Almost all writers are riddled with self-doubts, and when an idea is received by others with enthusiasm (as my camp story was), that can carry me a long way into the project. Some ideas can be killed by the intervention of others, and so you must choose judiciously with whom you share your ideas and how much you tell them. Many would-be writers make the mistake of talking out their ideas to the point that they lose all the energy for writing them. Ideally, you want to share your idea with someone who won't take it over, who doesn't have any hidden agendas or feel competitive with you, and who will offer just enough of a response to make you want to run to your writing desk and finish alone what s/he helped kick-start.

The Investigation

While all infiltrations are investigations of one sort or another, not all investigations are necessarily infiltrations. An investigator does not have to be either a spy or in insider in order to investigate. The investigator, in fact, operates in an uncomfortable zone between insider and outsider, and that tension is often what fuels and makes interesting the project.

A case in point: Geoff Dyer's attempt to write a critical biography of D. H. Lawrence. How can a biography be an immersion memoir? You only need to discover this delightfully frustrating book to see how. Dyer sets out to write a conventional book, but winds up writing a great work of procrastination. He researches the life of Lawrence exhaustively, rereads his novels and stories, and follows the ghost of Lawrence around the globe, traveling to the various spots where Lawrence lived. But the more obsessed he is with Lawrence, the less able he is to write about the great author—the book becomes an obsessive study of obsession and ambition itself, and writing the book about Lawrence becomes a kind of extended metaphor for all those projects we wish we could complete but never can. I love the book, but I know a number of people who can't get through it because it's such a frustrating read. I see Dyer's obsession as a bit of a pose, an exaggerated persona. That doesn't mean a persona is a lie, but we have many different aspects to our personalities, and often a writer will necessarily emphasize one aspect and exclude others to good effect. For some who have never written about themselves, this might be difficult to grasp, but most writers understand, I think, that we're constantly choosing what details about ourselves to include and what to exclude, whether this process is always conscious or not. We have to choose, or our books would never end. The portrait that emerges isn't dishonest, or any more dishonest than any combination of words on a page. It's possible to be completely honest about yourself and at the same time selective and manipulative in the details you choose for the sake of keeping the prose focused and moving at a readable pace. That's the contradiction and beauty of art.

I've had the opportunity to meet Dyer, and to spend a little time over the course of several days with him. When I met him, he was a good twelve years beyond writing his nonbiography of D. H. Lawrence, *Out of Sheer Rage: Wrestling with D. H. Lawrence.* Dyer struck me as focused, witty, erudite, and sure-footed. Perhaps inside there lurks an insecure and self-obsessed pedant, but if he's there, he's kept well hidden on public occasions. Yet, he gallops hilariously and annoyingly through the pages of *Out of Sheer Rage.*

> I had made progress on my study, that is, I had made progress in my mental preparation but now I had stalled. My lassitude was irritating me a good deal and this meant that Rome irritated me a good deal, too. There had been several mornings when the Caffè Farnese had not had the *cornetti integrali* that I depended on for my breakfast. Without these *integrali*—more accurately *with* the disappointment of not having had my *integrali*—I found it difficult to get started on my work. I sulked, I went on a tacit strike as a protest against the Farnese and its undependable supply of *integrali*. I picked up books and put them down, thought about doing some writing and then did the washing up instead. I recognized all these signs of unfocused anxiety and began to wonder if it might not be a good idea to move somewhere else to write my study of Lawrence. (91)

But moving, of course, does no good either.

Obsession is a great place from which to start any investigation—any book at all, as a matter of fact. Most of the world's masterpieces are about one obsession or another. You might think that Dyer's obsession with Lawrence (and self-obsession) was a one-off, that there couldn't be many books of this sort. But that's not exactly the case—an investigation/obsession with an author or artist or public figure is a growing subgenre. Nicholson Baker, in his book *U & I,* describes in amusing detail his youthful obsession with John Updike. Elizabeth Hawes, in *Camus, A Romance,* writes of her forty-year investigation of the famous existential writer Albert Camus. As with Dyer and Baker, Hawes becomes a private investigator who sifts through the layers of her own identity by exploring another's. She uncovers every bit of Camus trivia possible to uncover (his love of ping-pong, the fact that he wrote standing up), interviews his daughter, and eventually smudges out a word by mistake on one of his original manuscripts, becoming a fascinating literary stalker whose identity begins to merge with his.

Happily for the fledgling immersion writer's sense of mental wellbeing, an investigation does not necessary entail losing yourself and merging with the personality of the object of your investigation. You can retain a smidgeon of your dignity and self-control and still write a good book.

In *Green Fields: Crime, Punishment, and a Boyhood Between*, author Bob Cowser Jr. returns to a crime from his youth, the 1979 rape and murder of one of his elementary school classmates, Cary Ann Medlin, in the rural Tennessee town of Greenfield, where he grew up. When he began his investigation, Cary Ann's murderer had already been executed for the crime, and Cary Ann had been dead for decades. So, what was left to investigate, we might wonder. To me, the book is an investigation into the human heart as well as an investigation into childhood, parenthood, and inevitable loss. It's also an eloquent investigation of mercy. The book begins with an epigraph from one of my favorite short stories, "Death in the Woods," by Sherwood Anderson. In the story, the narrator recounts the story of an old, mistreated woman in rural Ohio who freezes to death on her long walk from town back to her farm. Her death has haunted the narrator for much of his life, and he delves back into it, investigates it, in order to locate its meaning for him. That's a more sophisticated kind of investigation than simply a "whodunit." Even after we know the bare facts of a crime or accident, questions inevitably linger—we try to make sense out of the senseless, at least writers do. I discuss in my own Turning Life into Fiction the passage in which Anderson writes:

> The scene in the forest had become for me, without my knowing it, the foundation for the real story I am now trying to tell. The fragments, you see, had to be picked up slowly, long afterwards. The whole thing . . . was to me as I grew older like music heard from far off. The notes had to be picked up slowly, one at a time. Something had to be understood. (244)

The same is true for Cowser's investigation. As I read the book, I felt in me a rising panic (as the father of four daughters) as he investigated this decades-old crime and described the harrowing events surrounding Cary Ann's abduction and murder. What makes the book immersion memoir, and what makes it especially sad and beautiful, is Cowser's personal investment in the story. No, he wasn't a close friend of Cary Ann's—he had some memories of her, but they shared a space, a place, a youth, and hers ended while Cowser traveled on. When he ventures down to Tennessee to investigate Cary Ann's murder, the court clerks are of course surprised to see him. Most everyone involved in the case is dead, even the investigators, and what good will it do? Cary Ann isn't coming back. But as any memoirist knows, actually she *is* coming back. Any writer writing about the past is recovering the dead, is Orpheus leading Eurydice from Hades. In the Greek myth, Orpheus makes the mistake of glancing back, thus condemning his love to the underworld instead of rescuing her. Backward glances are almost always bad in such tales. Think of Lot's wife! For the memoirist, the backward glance is in itself what saves. What might seem at first hopeless is actually a gesture of love and recovery. The writer forces herself to look, not to turn away, in order to recover something that the rest of us need, but don't know we need, and might not at first want to see or acknowledge: human frailty itself. Cowser forces himself and us to look:

> I laid the envelope in front of myself on the desk in the small library cubicle and opened its brads, then slid the large prints from inside and laid them before me on the table. The girl in the pictures looked almost exactly as I'd remembered her, yet unmistakably dead, splayed awkwardly in the weeds. John Everett Millais's drowned Ophelia, only bone-dry. I thought of the last time I'd seen her, through the chain link fence of the University Courts swimming pool. "What are you doing here?" she'd called out. It was a good question, then and now. I went to lunch and ordered a plate of food but couldn't eat a bite. I drove the rental car the fifty miles to my parents' house where I was spending the night and brought the photocopies I'd made inside with me. Only my mother would look, still determined, I think, to protect me. (39)

The investigation is very much a personal one, though the implications are larger in that the book also makes an eloquent appeal against the death penalty. Still, the investigation that most matters is that of Cowser's childhood and beliefs, the person he was allowed to grow up to be.

Unwittingly, I had a little bit of a hand in the genesis of this project when I was a visiting professor at St. Lawrence University. That semester, Bob was in the middle of another immersion project. A former college football player, he had recently tried out for and had been accepted as a player on America's oldest semiprofessional football team, the Watertown Red and Black, extant since 1895. The resulting book, *Dream Season: A Professor Joins America's Oldest Semi-Pro Football Team*, rightfully garnered a lot of positive attention. We were out having a drink, chatting about the book as well as an essay he'd written about Cary Ann Medlin and her murderer, and about his feelings on capital punishment. He'd asked me to comment on the essay, and I don't remember much about the meeting except that I thought the essay was too short, that there was a lot more he could say on the subject. But Bob credits me with asking one crucial question: "What does her mother think now?"

He says the question launched him into his investigation. Not only did he eventually read four thousand pages of trial transcripts, but he spoke with Cary Ann's mother and was able to find out what she thought pretty quickly. Within two minutes of making contact with her, she asked him what he thought of the death penalty. He knew this was her litmus test, that his answer would determine whether or not she would cooperate with him. He also knew the answer she wanted from him, but it wasn't the answer he could give. It wasn't the honest answer, and so he told her he was against the death penalty. After that, she gave him rote answers to his questions, the type of information he could as easily glean from newspaper accounts. She shut down. Still, Bob thinks in a way her lack of cooperation freed him from being beholden to her version of events. From that point on, he expended his efforts on interviews with others surrounding the case, those who would talk to him, as well as his own conjecture, his own imagination, what the story meant to him. From that point on, he owned the story he wanted to tell, and that's something worth stressing. No matter what the subject, you don't want to be someone else's mouthpiece. Your immersion narrative will be compelling to read only if you have full ownership of the story.

There's always more than one side to a story, as the truism goes. It's also true that there are many ways to tell a story, a seemingly infinite variety at times—in itself a sometimes overwhelming, writer's-block-inducing prospect. If the questions you're wrestling with are ultimately personal questions (how *do* I feel about the death penalty? for instance), then immersion memoir is your best bet, most likely. If, on the other hand, you see yourself as the stand-in, a convenient body double, as it were, for the reader, then your project might be best understood as a work of immersion journalism.

While the journalist at least attempts objectivity, there's no such constraint upon the memoirist. Imagine a journalist attending the parole hearing of the person who murdered her sister and trying to write a traditional article about the hearing. If the journalist left out the *I* in such a piece, she would not only be lying to the public in effect, but also to herself. In *Bereft: A Sister's Story*, Jane Bernstein tells the story of her older sister, Laura, who was murdered at age twenty in 1966 after transferring to Arizona State University to be close to her fiancé. The facts of the case are simple and stark: As Laura Bernstein was chaining her bicycle in an alley behind the Casa Loma Hotel in Tempe, only ten days after arriving in town, a young man came out of the dark and stabbed her four times in the torso and twice in the head. Eventually, the man confessed and was sent to prison for life.

Laura's sister, Martha (as Jane Bernstein was known then), hardly spoke Laura's name again for eight years—in fact, she hardly spoke her own name again. Eleven months after the murder, Martha took her middle name, *Jane*, and left *Martha* behind. Although the sisters had been close (Laura had asked Martha to be her bridesmaid), Jane got on with her life with hardly a backward glance. Partly, this was because of her parents, especially her mother, who thought silence the healthiest cure for grief. Getting on with one's life meant not facing one's life. And so, Martha and Laura were left in the past. Not until nearly a quarter of a century had passed did Jane Bernstein start sifting through the facts of her sister's murder to begin a conventional detective story (why was her sister killed?) and a personal detective story (who had Jane become since her sister's murder, and why?).

First, Bernstein writes, she had to admit to herself "that I had a sister. Then I spoke her name aloud. Laura, I said. It was as if I were calling out to her and she was answering me, for I began to dream about her all the time. By then it was 1974, and eight years had passed since the murder" (132).

The central concern in this book is the idea that one has to confront one's past in order to move on; one can't simply shut one's eyes as Bernstein's parents did, and hope one's wounds will miraculously heal themselves. And so, Bernstein must not only admit she had a sister whom she loved, but she must face other difficult emotional truths as well. She leaves a marriage to a man whose frequent rages and occasional physical violence paralyze her and her children. She not only admits she had a sister, but tries to reconstruct her death, tries even to understand her sister's killer.

Eventually, she visits the crime scene with the original detective who worked on the case. She speaks at the parole hearings of her sister's murderer and single-handedly prevents his release, not out of vengeance but because he had shut his eyes on his crime and couldn't even remember Laura's name:

> "All he currently recalls is that it was at night and a girl was riding her bicycle past him and she 'bumped' into him as she passed," it said in a report.
>
> How could you know your own heart if you turned away so fast? I wondered as I read that. If you could not find the source of your anger or despair, what good were any promises that the future would be any different from the past? How was it possible to know what you felt if you were foolish enough to believe that shutting your eyes would make something go away and never come back? (216)

In a way, most memoirs are detective stories in that it's the memoirist's unenviable task to sift through the crimes of the past and try to assign culpability. Often the blame rests on the memoirist's own shoulders, or if not blame exactly, at least a kind of personal responsibility for the past that he or she has not been able to face until now. But in some cases, the memoirist must actually return to the scene, as it were, and affect changes not only in her own life, but in the lives of others as well, including her readers.

The Quest

A quest suggests a journey, but there certainly are quests that are not so much about travel as about personal goals. Actually, all quests are, by definition, about personal goals, but some don't involve travel. The word *quest* comes from old French, from the thirteenth-century *queste*, the act of seeking. The connotation of knights off on a ramble in search of the Holy Grail and other such wonders didn't appear until the fourteenth century. If such factoids appeal to you, then you might be interested in the quests of A. J. Jacobs and Ammon Shea. I love such tidbits of relatively irrelevant information, but I possess neither the stamina nor the sustained curiosity to read the entire *Encyclopedia Britannica* from *A* to *Z* as A. J. Jacobs did in *The Know-it-All: One Man's Humble Quest to Become the Smartest Man in the World* or the entire *Oxford English Dictionary*, as Ammon Shea did in *Reading the OED: One Man, One Year, 21,730 pages*.

In order for a quest to be of interest, it's got to be a bit cockamamy and it's got to be difficult. No one really wants to read about an easy quest. You probably won't find a publisher for *Jittery: One Man's Quest to Quadruple his Daily Consumption of Caffeine and Live* or *The Year of Three's Company: One Man's Quest to Watch Every Episode and Stay Sane*. But who am I to say? There have been some pretty odd and gimmicky quest memoirs written over the last several years, and the fact that I won't read them isn't necessarily a gauge of their potential popularity. *Jittery*, in the hands of the right author, could become an instant classic. Jacobs and Shea are witty and smart (obviously) writers—without wit and inventiveness and the ability to glean the most amazing anecdotes from their respective mammoth reference books, imagine how tedious such slogs might be. Shea breaks up his memoir into twenty-six chapters, one for each letter of the alphabet, extracting the most unusual words from thousands, along with his accompanying wry commentary—the book is carried by its eccentric commentary as well as the eccentric nature of the quest. An example is the word *acnestis*: "On an animal the point of the back that lies between the shoulders and the lower back, which cannot be reached to be scratched." Of *acnestis*, Shea comments:

> I am very glad I found this word early in my reading of the *O.E.D.*—the fact that there existed a word for this thing which previously I had been sure lacked a name was such a delight to me that suddenly the whole idea of reading the dictionary seemed utterly reasonable. (6)

A. J. Jacobs, whose book preceded Shea's by a couple of years, takes a similar approach, dividing his exploration of the encyclopedia alphabetically, though he's much more revealing about his personal life, casting his wife, Julie, as a reluctant sidekick in his quest (she takes to fining him one dollar for every irrelevant fact he spouts) and portraying himself as an increasingly annoying nerd (all with characteristic charm and wit).

Both Jacobs and Shea arrived at their odd ambitions honestly. Jacobs's dad attempted to read the encyclopedia when Jacobs was in high school, but only got as far as the Bs, And Shea apparently has long been a devotee of dictionaries (twenty-one of twenty-five boxes he carried with him from one apartment to another contained them). I think that's a point worth stressing. I am *not* a devotee of either dictionaries or the encyclopedia—I have a casual interest in them, but a casual interest is not enough to make a book. That's the difference between a gimmick and a book with something at stake. If you don't have a true investment in your idea, your readers won't either. It's called "phoning it in," and we've all run across teachers and writers who phone it in, who have become so bored and world-weary that they've lost their emotional and intellectual investment in the work they used to love.

Quests involve physical toil as well as mental, of course. One such quest book is W. Hodding Carter's *Off the Deep End: The Probably Insane Idea that I Could Swim My Way through a Midlife Crisis—and Qualify for the Olympics*. When Carter was a student at Kenyon College, he had been a champion swimmer, but he failed to qualify for the

Olympics. So, at the age of forty-five, he decides to take another shot at his youthful goal and he begins to train in earnest, swimming six days a week, often with weights, swimming around Manhattan, training with his old college coach, and even besting his old personal records. Going into the book, we know he probably won't qualify, though he does a pretty good job of convincing us that he might. We learn that he's ranked number one in the country in his age group, and forty-five doesn't seem *that* old (okay, it's old). But forty-one-year-old Dara Torres *did* qualify for the 2008 Olympics, and won three silver medals (to go with her collection of golds and others from previous Olympics), making her my hero and the hero of most middle-aged men and women. The point is that we root for Carter, or at least I do. Some people would say, oh just grow up, accept the fact that you're getting old. But the people who accept things as they are tend not to write books. Books involve conflict and complaint and dissatisfaction. Aging and dying are two conflicts we all share.

A physical quest doesn't always involve some kind of sport. In the case of Paula Kamen's *All in My Head*, the quest involved trying to relieve herself of the pain of a chronic headache. A book about someone trying to lose weight or gain weight might be considered a quest, though in the case of filmmaker Morgan Spurlock in *Super Size Me*, it was definitely more of an experiment. It wasn't his *quest* to balloon in weight in thirty days by eating piles of junk. That would simply be mad, a suicide attempt, and we'd have to classify it as a train wreck. No, a quest book has to possess at least a modicum of earnestness—the writer must truly want the end result. Spurlock went on a diet following his experiment, but Jacobs really wanted to read the encyclopedia and Shea wanted to read the *OED*, and Carter wanted to challenge his physical limitations. Kamen certainly wanted to cure her headache.

Exercises

1. Make a list of ten things you'd like to do over. Some of these activities would probably be impossible to redo, but not all of them. Narrow

down the list to what's possible, but more importantly, narrow it down to the do-overs in which you would be most emotionally invested. Try it! Whether you publish it or not is secondary—the impact of revisiting the past and reinhabiting it will be lasting and hopefully positive.

2. Can you imagine embarking on a quest that doesn't involve travel? A task? A project? A goal or resolution that's always eluded you? The harder the task, the better. And again, it should be something for which you can identify some emotional stakes, though that doesn't necessarily mean it should be emotionally overwhelming. Maybe your quest is to clean out the garage or attic. It might seem simple, but wait until you start poring through those old photos and letters, knowing that you can't hold on to everything.

3. Embark on an investigation of something that's haunted you for a while. In this case, the investigation should be something that has some relevance to your life, not merely a mystery that intrigues you, which would be better suited for immersion journalism. Again, emotionally dangerous territory! Maybe you'll want to investigate the real reason your grandparents divorced. Or you might want to investigate a person, someone you've been obsessed with forever—I'm not suggesting you stalk someone. The person doesn't even have to be alive. Maybe you're a fervent Michael Jackson fan, and you find one of his white gloves for sale on eBay. Write about your obsession with that glove. The further you take us into your obsession and your reasons for this obsession, the better.

4. There's nothing more immersive than a blog. Try writing a blog for a month in which you engage in a project and report on it. This can be anything from a reenactment (as chronicled in *Julie and Julia*) to an experiment. The writer Ron Tanner and his wife, Jill, for example, bought a four-thousand-plus-square-foot Victorian brownstone in Baltimore, Maryland, that had been trashed by a fraternity, and turned it into a showpiece. Their blog, Houselove.org, not only chronicles their trials and triumphs refurbishing the house, but also provides a resource for other DIY-ers. Blogs are great ways to test-run your obsession.

5. Times have changed since the days of Frank Cushing's life with the Zuni. Such an experiment would likely seem outdated and presumptuous now, at the very least. But let's imagine such a project in a larger sense. What other culture might you adopt to learn about? Maybe you could be adopted by the culture of the bowling alley. Or the avid fan of . . . a sport . . . a musician . . . a game . . . a hobby. Of course, such an experiment is ripe for parody and could get a little silly if you're not careful, and that's okay, but see if you can play it with a straight face, if you can approach the society you're infiltrating with an open mind and a desire to learn. It will probably be more interesting than only going for the easy laugh. Remember, this is also about chronicling your own doubts and fears, and that could be fun and insightful, depending upon how different the group you're writing about is from you.

Chapter Two

Immersion Journalism

Memoir does not require the memoirist to venture outside into the world. There are plenty of memoirists who spend their days simply writing about the long-ago past. But most journalism requires a certain amount of immersion in the outside world, though I've heard about (but never encountered) journalists who sit by a pool all day in some exotic locale and leave the legwork to others while immersing themselves in the hot tub. Let's be clear that for writers other than these mythic journalists, there's a certain amount of immersion involved in simply chasing down a story, in interviewing the people involved and in visiting the sites of the story. But if the journalist leaves herself out of the story, it's not an immersion piece. Some writers simply do not feel comfortable being included in the story. Think of many, though not all, of the essays of Joan Didion or John McPhee. Some writers and readers prefer writing that doesn't call obvious attention to the writer, except in the artfulness of the prose and the precision of the details. But the immersion journalist consciously makes herself a part of the story.

Another name for immersion journalism is *participatory journalism*. Whatever you call the work, this type of writer engages in the activity he or she wants to write about in order to get an insider's look at the subject. Sometimes such projects are dismissed as "stunt journalism," but in the best such examples, there's far more than a stunt being performed, though some such books do have an element of whimsy and playfulness.

A pioneer of the form, unafraid to *be* the story, was the laudable and fearless Nellie Bly, who looms large in my personal pantheon of immersion heroes. Her real name was Elizabeth Jane Cochrane; she took on the pseudonym of Nellie Bly at a time when the idea of a female reporter was both novel and somewhat scandalous. Almost no one can compare to her in terms of what she was willing to do to report a story. She essentially invented immersion journalism, first posing as a sweatshop worker to expose the appalling conditions under which women toiled in her hometown of Pittsburgh in the 1880s. Later, in New York, working for the *New York World*, she feigned insanity to have herself committed to the women's lunatic asylum on Blackwell's Island. In both cases, she caused a storm of controversy. Perhaps her crowning piece of immersion reportage was her successful attempt to travel around the world in fewer than eighty days, in emulation of the Jules Verne novel *Around the World in 80 Days*. She did it in seventy-two, besting a female reporter from a rival paper who was traveling in the opposite direction.

But let's focus on her courageous decision to have herself committed to a mental hospital. Certainly, the stunt of traveling around the world in less than eighty days seems like a project that would be much more fun than committing yourself to a squalid 1880s New York lunatic asylum. And while there was physical risk involved in the Jules Verne stunt, that's what it was basically: a stunt, with less at risk emotionally than the asylum project. Physical risk can be terrifying, but emotional risk can be doubly so. At least, if you put yourself in harm's way physically, there's a chance you can be rescued, but who can rescue you from the uncharted and dangerous waters of your own mind? And no one could enter into such a project without at least flirting with mental instability, as Nellie Bly learned. It was one thing for her to make grotesque faces in front of the mirror in preparation for her role, but when she deprived herself of sleep at a working class boarding house and feigned paranoia in front of her fellow boarders, she frightened not only them but herself as well. There was something more at stake than simply selling papers, and the project had a certain nobility about it that the around-the-world stunt, as exciting as it is, lacks. Here, she wanted to learn the truth about conditions in the asylums. She was on the side of the patients. The night she began her project, she alarmed the inhabitants of the boarding house she had chosen by stating that they all looked crazy and that she was afraid they might murder her. She also feigned amnesia. By the end of the evening, she'd convinced them that *she* was the crazy one and that she might murder *them* by morning. No one wanted to be near her except for one kind woman, a proofreader from Boston named Mrs. Caine:

No one wanted to be responsible for me, and the woman who was to occupy the room with me declared that she would not stay with that "crazy woman" for all the money of the Vanderbilts. It was then that Mrs. Caine said she would stay with me. I told her I would like to have her do so. So she was left with me. She didn't undress, but lay down on the bed, watchful of my movements. She tried to induce me to lie down, but I was afraid to do this. I knew that if I once gave way I should fall asleep and dream as pleasantly and peacefully as a child. I should, to use a slang expression, be liable to "give myself dead away." So I insisted on sitting on the side of the bed and staring blankly at vacancy. My poor companion was put into a wretched state of unhappiness. Every few moments she would rise up to look at me. She told me that my eyes shone terribly brightly and then began to question me, asking me where I had lived, how long I had been in New York, what I had been doing, and many things besides. To all her questionings I had but one response—I told her that I had forgotten everything, that ever since my headache had come on I could not remember.

Poor soul! How cruelly I tortured her, and what a kind heart she had! But how I tortured all of them! One of them dreamed of me—as a nightmare. After I had been in the room an hour or so, I was myself startled by hearing a woman screaming in the next room. I began to imagine that I was really in an insane asylum.

Mrs. Caine woke up, looked around, frightened, and listened. She then went out and into the next room, and I heard her asking another woman some questions. When she came back she told me that the woman had had a hideous nightmare. She had been dreaming of me. She had seen me, she said, rushing at her with a knife in my hand, with the intention of killing her. In trying to escape me she had fortunately been able to scream, and so to awaken herself and scare off her nightmare. Then Mrs. Caine got into bed again, considerably agitated, but very sleepy.

I was weary, too, but I had braced myself up to the work, and was determined to keep awake all night so as to carry on my work of impersonation to a successful end in the morning. I heard midnight. I had yet six hours to wait for daylight. The time passed with excruciating slowness. Minutes appeared hours. The noises in the house and on the avenue ceased.

Fearing that sleep would coax me into its grasp, I commenced to review my life. How strange it all seems! One incident, if never so trifling, is but a link more to chain us to our unchangeable fate. I began at the beginning, and lived again the story of my life. Old friends were recalled with a pleasurable thrill; old enmities, old heartaches, old joys were once again present. The turned-down pages of my life were turned up, and the past was present.

When it was completed, I turned my thoughts bravely to the future, wondering, first, what the next day would bring forth, then making plans for the carrying out of my project. I wondered if I should be able to pass over the river to the goal of my strange ambition, to become eventually an inmate of the halls inhabited by my mentally wrecked sisters. And then, once in, what would be my experience? And after? How to get out? Bah! I said, they will get me out.

That was the greatest night of my existence. For a few hours I stood face to face with "self!" (http://digital.library.upenn.edu/women/bly/madhouse/madhouse.html)

That last sentence stuns me a bit because I recognize it, this standing face to face with self. But it's not so much the type of sentiment a journalist typically expresses; more the sentiment of a memoirist. One of the chief privileges of memoir, one of its goals, is a kind of archeological dig, an excavation of the layers of self so that you can see yourself honestly for who you are, not in terms of moral judgments, good or bad, necessarily, but who you are in terms of the person you've become as a result of the experiences that have formed your life. It must have been a harrowing night for Nellie Bly, this sifting through her life, because her childhood was not a happy one. Her father, an associate judge, died when she was a young girl. He left no will and she and her mother were forced to leave their home and their belongings were auctioned off. Soon after, her mother remarried, but the marriage was an unhappy one, and Nellie's stepfather was violent and abusive. So that night of facing her Self frankly must have been a difficult one indeed. There must have been times in her youth when she felt the helplessness of being trapped in a world that seemed deranged. Well, of course this makes sense. Nellie Bly was an uncommonly brave person, brave enough to look at herself stripped bare and consider it the greatest night of her life.

Nellie Bly lived in a prepsychoanalytic world. A contemporary writer probably could not get away with saying, "I came face to face with self," and leave it at that, though there are plenty of people who would happily still leave it at that. Why be burdened by someone else's personal demons (the argument goes), by someone else's self-indulgent whining? I wouldn't want Nellie Bly's exposé to be anything other than what it is, nor could it be. This wasn't meant to be a memoir, but knowing something of her context, the struggles of her early life, gives an added dimension to our understanding of Nellie Bly, even if we have to supply this information on our own.

Among the more well-known contemporary examples of the form is Barbara Ehrenreich's *Nickel and Dimed*, in which the author took a series of minimum-wage jobs to demonstrate just how difficult it is for many working-class Americans to get by. In the process of doing her research, Ehrenreich worked as a housecleaner, a restaurant server, a nursing home aide, a housemaid, and a Walmart associate. In doing so, she was able to create a personal narrative that made her point much more eloquently and entertainingly than any number of statistics and news articles on unemployment and underemployment in America.

I can hardly express this point strongly enough. The writer of such an investigation becomes the stand-in for the countless souls whose everyday existence she is investigating. Our minds are captivated by the stories of individuals, not multitudes, and for this reason, the stark number of six million is impenetrable and unfathomable compared to the story of one young girl, Anne Frank, murdered by the Nazis.

Ehrenreich's is but one example of the many fine works of participatory journalism that have been written. Another such book is Ted Conover's *Newjack*, for which the journalist spent a year as a prison guard at Sing Sing prison. This kind of immersion journalism gives us insights that no other means of reportage could ever hope to accomplish. It's one thing to interview prisoners and prison officials on the ways in which prison dehumanizes both inmates and guards; it's quite another to *become* one of those guards in order to experience this process first-hand. Conclusions are hard-won, but nearly unassailable. You can see what I mean in this short passage from the book, in which Conover muses on exactly this point, that doing the job brings revelations that simply hearing about the job cannot convey:

> Back at the academy, more than one instructor had said it took four or five years to make a good CO. I had wondered why. There had seemed to be no difficult concepts to master; the rules were all straightforward. In terms of civil service, you were only on probation for a year. The easiest way to get in trouble, everyone said, was to arrive at work late or call in sick too often. The four or five years thing had sounded like self-flattery.
>
> But after five months at Sing-Sing, I understood. Experience mattered. Or, more precisely, it took time (and confrontations) to decide (or to discover) what kind of person was going to be wearing your uniform. A hard-ass or a softie? Inmates' friend or inmates' enemy? Straight or crooked? A user of force or a writer of tickets? A strict overseer or a lender of hands? The job was full of discretionary power and the decisions about how to use it were often moral. (249)

Conover's prose is straightforward and clearheaded. The old journalistic virtue of supposed objectivity is replaced by the more reasonable notion that an honest personal account is not only more readable than an old-school human-interest feature on Sing Sing prison, but more thoroughly researched and more trustworthy. Any journalist who endures a year as a prison guard has instant credibility, as far as I'm concerned.

While Barbara Ehrenreich and Ted Conover might well learn more about themselves through the tasks they've taken on, their primary interests are sociological and journalistic. What makes one immersion work a memoir and another a journalistic piece depends largely on the aims of the project. Is the goal to discover something about oneself or to discover something about the world? Not that the two are mutually exclusive. It's a matter of degree.

In the mid-1990s I lived in Bellingham, Washington, and my friend David Shields was working on his book *Black Planet: Facing Race During an NBA Season*. His idea was to watch every home game of the Seattle Supersonics (actually, he wanted to go on the road with them, too, but he couldn't get permission from the team, so he settled for being an ordinary fan) and take a look at white fans' fascination with black players as a way of examining race issues. It was an edgy idea, but David is full of edgy ideas. In the course of writing the book, he exaggerated and conflated a few things. He went to the games with several friends, including myself, but he combined us all into one friend (not physically, thankfully, which would have been awkward) for the sake of the fluidity of the narrative. Before you call out the Truth Police, take a few breaths. It's no big deal. Nothing meaningful in the course of events was distorted—not to my knowledge, at any rate. He also exaggerated his fascination with one player in particular, Gary Peyton, turning this fascination into an obsession for the sake of his theme. It was a smart and courageous look at a subject that a lot of people didn't want to examine frankly, and he was lambasted by a few reviewers in ways that seemed to me more indicative of their problems than his. A couple of reviewers seemed to be taking out their own racial anxieties on David in their neurotic reviews. In other words, he touched a nerve. Bingo. Just what good writers do. One reviewer in particular wrote nastily that Americans might be screwed up about race, but at least they weren't as screwed up as David Shields. If I had been attacked in that way, I would have folded into the fetal position. But David calmly and intelligently wrote an essay in the *New York Times* in which he detailed how, in writing *Black Planet,* he was using himself as a conduit for the larger culture's neuroses. His bottom line: my neuroses are your neuroses. I'm sure of it.

A good immersion journalist is almost always a stand-in for a culture's obsessions and anxieties. In my case, I became intrigued with a story I had heard of in the 1990s, the story of a purported anthropological hoax in the Philippines: the Tasaday tribe.

The Tasaday were a band of twenty-six men, women, and children who were living in the rainforest of the southern Philippines when they were "discovered" living in complete isolation by a hunter named Dafal. The hunter told his story of meeting this group of forest dwellers to a local chieftain named Mai Tuan, who then passed along the information to the Philippine government minister in charge of national minorities, Manuel Elizalde, a controversial playboy and member of one of the Philippines' elite families. Once Elizalde was involved, the story of the Tasaday mushroomed overnight. Within days, journalists and anthropologists were visiting these shy forest dwellers, and they became instant celebrities, eventually gracing the cover of *National Geographic* and serving as the subject of various documentaries worldwide.

The remarkable thing about the Tasaday was that they lived a kind of stone-age existence in complete isolation, though they had neighbors within several miles as the crow flies. They resided in caves, had no word for *war* or *weapon* (very important to a world bloodied by war in Vietnam and other conflicts, including the ever-simmering Cold War), seemed to dwell in perfect harmony with nature, had no cloth, wore only leaves, possessed no metal, and used only stone tools. A forty-five-thousand-acre reserve was soon declared for them in the rainforest to protect them from unscrupulous loggers and miners who would just as soon kill them as deal with them. Over the next several years, Elizalde carefully controlled the visitors who entered the Tasaday Manobo Reserve. In 1975, he decided to close the reserve to visitors, claiming that the Tasaday should be left in peace. For the next twelve years, no one visited the Tasaday until the overthrow of the Marcos dictatorship in 1986, when an enterprising Swiss reporter named Oswald Iten hiked unannounced into the rainforest in the company of a

Filipino reporter and activist, Joey Lozano. The pair found the Tasaday in jeans and T-shirts, a couple toting rifles. Where were the so-called gentle Tasaday? Iten was told through interpreters that they had been a figment of Manuel Elizalde's imagination: simple farmers who had been bribed and coerced into pretending to be cave dwellers.

Delighted by this scoop, Iten hiked out of the rainforest and promptly filed his story, which ignited an immediate worldwide controversy. The tribe had been transformed overnight from the ethnographic find of the century to the ethnographic fraud of the century. Over the next few years, several anthropological conferences devoted all or part of their sessions to the question of the Tasaday's authenticity. The results were inconclusive on both sides. The hoax proponents and those who insisted the Tasaday were "authentic" squared off, full of derision and contempt for one another.

Into this morass, I naively stepped, thinking like most people that the Tasaday were a simple and bald hoax, the conventional wisdom fueled by several sensationalized TV reports, including a widely viewed ABC 20/20 report called "The Tribe that Never Was."

But the truth wasn't so simple, I soon found out, after only a bit of digging. The project that I thought would take me two or three years at most eventually claimed five years of my writing life. Along the way, I traveled across the world, meeting with journalists, anthropologists, linguists, virtually everyone who had been involved in the story (excluding Elizalde, who had passed away a couple of weeks before I began my project), including the Tasaday themselves. Twice. I went to see the Tasaday in the volatile southern Philippines first with the hoax proponents, and then, six months later, with the authenticity proponents. My experiences were quite distinct in each case, and it was in part for this reason that I decided to include myself in the book. I felt and still feel that the story of the Tasaday was a story about perception and ambiguity, and that so much depended on your preconceptions, on *confirmation bias*. This is the idea I mentioned earlier that people tend to accept evidence that supports their preconceptions, while ignoring evidence that contradicts their assumptions.

The story wasn't about me, but it involved me, and I wanted readers to experience my own process of discovery as I navigated this strange narrative.

The only way to complete such a book is to become obsessed by it, and obsessed I was. The first draft I handed in to my editor was a whopping eight hundred pages. Happily, he didn't kick me out of his office and tell me never to darken his doorstep again. Instead, he told me to cut the book in half and come back in a year. The resulting book is very much a work of immersion journalism, a work not about the author but quite clearly experienced by a central protagonist.

As in any kind of immersion project, you have to understand that this will involve a dedicated commitment of time and energy. Depending on your project, it could also involve some risk, and you have to be prepared for that. At the outset of my project on the Tasaday, I was alarmed when I read on the Internet accounts of tourists and others being kidnapped in lawless Mindanao, where I was headed. The U.S. state department had issued a travel advisory, and Muslim separatists, most notably the Abu Sayyaf terrorist group, had recently kidnapped a group of European tourists at a resort in nearby Malaysia. Add to that a simmering civil war between the army and the Moro Islamic Liberation Front, and I began to wonder just what I had signed up for. I called my editor and told her the situation, figuring there must be some kind of secret publishers' slush fund made up of pooled-together returns of advances from writers with cold feet, and that these funds were used to get other more daring authors out of trouble. "What happens if I'm kidnapped?" I asked.

"We will lodge a very strong formal protest with the authorities," she said.

Very strong? Well, that was a relief. If the immersion memoir often entails the possibility of emotional damage, immersion journalism often entails physical duress as well. Several months after signing my contract, I found myself in a little village in the mountains of Mindanao being held at gunpoint. As I sat at the side of a thatched hut with an affable young man lazily training his ArmaLite rifle on me, I thought of warning him that he would soon be on the receiving end of a very strong protest from my publisher. And then . . . well, watch out, buddy!

But it wouldn't have done much good, as he spoke no English. Fortunately, my kidnapping lasted only a few hours, and no strong protests were necessary.

But if you insist on this foolhardy way of writing about politics, cultures, and society, don't let me dissuade you.

The Investigation

Most forms of immersion journalism involve some sort of investigation, though some are more investigative in nature than others, and it's these I'd like to focus on here. As with any such project, make sure that you want to devote a good portion of your life to your proposed investigation, because that's what you will be doing, if you want to write a worthwhile investigation. Obsession helps in this case, but it's not an absolute prerequisite. In my experience, if you're curious by nature, obsession can grow over time. I wasn't obsessed with the Tasaday when I first encountered the story, merely curious and intrigued. But as I interviewed more and more of the people involved and heard compelling evidence on both sides, I not only found myself confused, but increasingly excited that I had stumbled upon something big, something about more than simply whether one small band of forest dwellers in the Philippines was authentic or not.

Some writers are more present in their investigations than others, but a work of immersion journalism inevitably tips its hand, shows us what's at stake for the author, why he or she thinks this project is vital to your understanding of what it means to be human. Sometimes the reader already knows, or thinks s/he knows, what's at stake: you go to a biography of Lincoln or Teddy Roosevelt because, presumably, you already find them intriguing subjects. You don't need or expect the writer to show himself when reading such a work. In fact, if he does show himself, you might hiss, "Come on, get back behind the curtain. We don't care about you. We only want to read about the great man." That's exactly what happened to Pulitzer-Prize-winning biographer Edmund Morris when he published his much-awaited authorized biography of Ronald Reagan, *Dutch,* undoubtedly the first and perhaps the last-ever immersion presidential biography. Morris was excoriated in reviews and by admirers of Reagan because he made the unprecedented choice to include fictional characters in the biography, including an Americanized version of himself (he was born in Kenya and grew up in South Africa) who's present at many of the formative and important episodes of Reagan's life. He chose this approach because, even after unprecedented access, Reagan still seemed a cipher. The flap copy for the book calls Reagan a man of "extraordinary power and mystery." That's one way of putting it.

Morris learned little from his many conversations with Reagan, who regaled him with tired and oft-repeated anecdotes. He learned next to nothing from Reagan's private diary, too, and eventually began to see Reagan as "a hollow man." His son Michael recalled how proud he was when Reagan came to his high school graduation, only to have his father look him squarely in the eye and introduce himself as if to a stranger. "Dad, it's me. Your son, Mike," the younger Reagan told his father.

Ronald Reagan's first wife, the actress Jane Wyman, once told a friend, "I'm so bored with him I'll either kill myself or kill him." Obviously, if there ever was a man born for the public spotlight, it was Reagan—but the private Reagan was nearly impossible to grasp, even by those who were closest to him. It takes a lot of chutzpah (some might say arrogance) to cast yourself in a great man or woman's biography, but I applaud the idea. I would not normally pick up a biography of Reagan, but this genre-bending investigation of Reagan's life was in many ways well ahead of its time, and the writer suffered as a result.

There are many reasons why the writer of an investigative book might want to put himself in as a character—the least of which is narcissism. I suspect that Morris felt much about Reagan as I felt about the "lost tribe," the Tasaday, in *Invented Eden*. How you looked at the tribe depended so much upon the viewer and your own personal, political, and cultural baggage. There's a lot of ambiguity in such an investigation—and sometimes ambiguity is a more truthful representation than an unequivocal answer. Were the Tasaday a hoax? No. Were they an authentic "stone-age tribe?" No. What kind of person was Ronald

Reagan? Well, like most of us, he was not the same person in all circumstances. There was his public persona, which all of us knew and either loved or hated, and there was his private persona, which almost no one knew, with the possible exception of Nancy Reagan. But I wouldn't even take bets on that.

Not only does Morris cast himself as a childhood friend in *Dutch*, but he also invents a vicious Hollywood gossip columnist — a brilliant device in many ways. By viewing Reagan from many angles, we're able to triangulate various opinions of the man and hopefully come to our own. The book for which Morris won the Pulitzer, a conventional biography of Teddy Roosevelt, needed no such innovative techniques because Roosevelt was conventionally knowable. Reagan wasn't.

The interplay of fictive elements in the book is in many ways brilliantly imitative of Reagan's own techniques. Reagan lived most fully in a world of make-believe, often confusing the two, sometimes mixing up a role he played as a Hollywood actor before entering politics with something he genuinely experienced. He did this many times, well before his diagnosis of Alzheimer's. When Jewish groups and others complained bitterly about his visit to a cemetery in Germany where Nazi officers were buried, he reacted with wounded pride. Hadn't he been present at the liberation of Buchenwald and seen with his very eyes electric fencing and barbed wire cut by Allied troops, freeing the wretched prisoners? he asked. Well, no, actually, he had merely seen footage of it. Such a man warrants no less than a biography in which fantasy and reality freely mix.

Dutch is an anomaly. A good rule of thumb is that the less topical the subject, the more you have to show us why we should care about your investigation. Sure, a good story helps a lot, but it's not always enough. We want to know what the stakes are, why you care. If you convincingly show us that, chances are we'll care, too.

A number of years ago the writer Jon Krakauer visited my local bookstore to promote his first book, *Into the Wild*. Granted, this book is not overtly the most immersive book he's written (that honor probably goes to his book *Into Thin Air*, in which he chronicled a disastrous climbing expedition to Mount Everest), but there's an element of immersion in this book worth noting. The book started as a magazine piece for *Outside* in which Krakauer investigated the death of an eccentric young man from a well-to-do family who cut up all his credit cards, changed his name, and decided to live off the grid in Alaska. Camping in an abandoned school bus, he one day ate the wrong plant, which slowly poisoned him. But the investigation that Krakauer embarked upon was not so much an investigation of his death as why such a young man would reject society and take such risks. By extension, the book was about this entire breed of young American male: adventurous, iconoclastic, self-destructive. In the book, Krakauer writes of other adventurers who were lost in the wilderness because of what others might deem foolhardiness.

At one point in his slideshow presentation, Krakauer showed us a photo of Christopher McCandless (in my memory, it's McCandless, though it might have been some other doomed adventurer chronicled in the book) raising his arms in a kind of victorious shout. The next slide showed us an almost identical shot of a much younger Jon Krakauer in the same pose from his attempt to climb Devil's Thumb in Alaska. This was a moment of marvelous timing on Krakauer's part and one I've never forgotten—he was showing us what made him embark upon this investigation in the first place. It wasn't simple curiosity. It was simply stated: "There but for the grace of God go I." And it was in part celebratory of McCandless's spirit—McCandless might have been foolhardy in some ways, but he was also an idealist, and Krakauer wasn't going to dismiss him as some crazy kid who deserved what he got. Clearly, Krakauer was proud and a little in awe of the crazy kid he once was, too.

One difficulty of writing any book of immersion journalism is figuring out the ratio of self to subject in your narrative. This isn't such a problem in immersion memoir, because we expect a fair amount of self-disclosure in memoir. Journalists of the traditional kind tend to be squeamish about too much self-disclosure. The impulse is considered self-indulgent and even worse, unprofessional. Personally, I don't buy that it's unprofessional in and of itself, but it can be so if there's no call for the journalist to be a part of the story. Imagine writing a traditional news story about a zoning commission meeting to decide whether a house could be split into a multifamily unit. You'd probably liven up the story if you included yourself in the narrative, but you'd also most likely be fired:

> I've seen the developer who owns the property on South Jenkins in the co-op a few times and out jogging. Every time I see him, I wonder if I should go up and confront him. He seems a decent enough sort, but why does he have to turn every property he owns into a neglected and overcrowded student dwelling? These thoughts course through my mind during the preceding zoning hearing, in which a homeowner asks the commission for a permit to build a fence on her corner lot, a potential sight impairment for traffic on the busy street. Her plea interests me less than the Johnson Street case, and so I put down my pen and forget to pay attention to the ruling on her fence application.

Actually, I think this would make a fun parody of an immersion piece.

While it might well be unprofessional for a journalist to insert herself in every type of news story she covers, it might be equally unprofessional to exclude herself from certain types of narratives, especially those that involve the writer's personal obsession.

Still, it can be a bit dicey for an immersion journalist to figure out just how immersed she wants to be. One way to figure this out might be to determine how much the reader will benefit by having an avatar on the page (you) leading him through the complex shoals of the story you want to tell. Put yourself in as much as necessary, but no more, and try to do it with a light touch.

Let's say you and a college friend take a trip to the island of Samoa in the South Pacific. While there, you meet a Peace Corps volunteer who tells you of a murder that happened a couple of years back in the neighboring island country of Tonga. A male Peace Corps volunteer murdered another volunteer by stabbing her twenty-two times, and in the aftermath of the crime, the Peace Corps hustled the man off the island. It's one of those stories you hear that intrigues you, but you file it away along with dozens of others. Ten years later, you're working as a journalist in New York, where you meet another writer who had once been stationed as a Peace Corps volunteer in Tonga. Has he heard of the murder? you ask. Yes, the story's well-known among Tonga volunteers. He thinks the victim's name was Elsa Mae Swenson. Curiosity piqued, you go to the library (this is before the days of the Google search) and locate the one article in the *New York Times* that appeared about the murder, which took place in October of 1976. The victim's name was Deborah Ann Gardner, a twenty-three-year-old teacher who had been stabbed to death by Dennis Priven, another volunteer, who faced a possible sentence of being hanged. A little more research uncovers a verdict of not guilty by reason of insanity. Priven is handed over to the U.S. on the condition that he's to be committed to a mental hospital. But two years after the murder, Priven's phone number is listed in the Manhattan phone directory. Maybe you're tempted to call. Maybe you do. A raspy voice answers and you hang up.

Still, you're not quite hooked. Then in 1997, a writer friend tells you he's been assigned by *Travel and Leisure* to experience the dawn of the new millennium in Tonga, the first place in the world that will see the sun rise. Tonga? Really? Well, isn't that a coincidence, and you tell him of this murder story you've been kicking around for over a decade. Stunned, your friend turns to you and asks why you're bothering to write anything else.

That's the way it happened for Philip Weiss, as he explains in his book *American Taboo: A Murder in the Peace Corps*. Sometimes it takes a decade or more for an idea to take hold. Sometimes all you need is someone else's enthusiasm. One friend of mine compares his many ideas for books to flirtatious women. When one idea flirts with him, he brushes it aside. You're not *really* interested in me, he thinks. But if the idea is insistent, if it keeps coming back and seems truly interested in his attention, not simply offering a mindless and wasteful distraction, then he warms up to it. I hasten to add that this is an equal opportunity metaphor. You may cast your flirtatious idea as male or female, gay or straight. The point is that time is a great test of any idea's worthiness. If you keep returning to it, or, if the cosmos seemingly keeps putting the idea in front of you, that might be a good indication that it's something worth pursuing.

Weiss deftly includes himself in his investigation where and when it's

useful to have himself present in the narrative, while at other times stepping aside and letting the story unfold. He conducts interviews with
everyone still alive who will speak with him, though not everyone will
do so, while others are impossible to locate. Deborah's mother, Alice,
has moved on and doesn't want to speak with him at first; Weiss is sympathetic, but tells her he plans to write the book anyway: it's a matter
of public record, and no one knows about the story, and it still haunts
a number of old Peace Corps volunteers. Some people are afraid to
talk to Weiss, while others insult him, call him a "muckraker." But once
Weiss is fully on the case, he attacks it with obsessive zeal. The story
is indeed sad and terrible, and it's hard to read it without feeling that
justice was not served. A beautiful and vivacious young woman was vi-
ciously killed and her murderer not only got away with it, but seems to
view his escape from justice as an "accomplishment," as Weiss tells us.

I first read the book when it appeared in 2004, and while I still retain
the bare facts of Gardner's murder, what's really etched in my mind is
the part of the book toward the end when Weiss spends a day walking
around Manhattan with the murderer. What I find most remarkable
about the book is how personal an investigation the murder becomes
for Weiss. He never knew Gardner, never knew any of the people involved, but by the end, it's as though Priven murdered his sister or fian-
cée. In no way is he a dispassionate journalistic observer, and if he had
written the story as such, it would hold absolutely no allure for me, or
very little. It's Weiss's passion and obsession that makes the story come
alive.

The scene of Weiss and Priven, the journalist and the murderer,
strolling around Manhattan is remarkable in part because Priven traps
Weiss in his own code of journalistic ethics, agreeing to talk to him
only if Weiss agrees that everything he says will be off the record. And
so, Weiss is stuck and can only report his side of the conversation, but
that's revealing enough, especially when he relates to Priven a dream he
had after meeting Deborah's mother:

> I told him about the dream that had gotten me going: The night after I
> met Deb's mother and told her that I was writing this book, I was awak-

ened by a dream. I was carrying two pairs of hiking boots away from an auction house where I had left them, to be sold to others. Now they were mine again, and filled with ice. Someone tried to stop me from taking them away, but I brought the boots back to my house and set them by the fireplace and set a big book to burning in the fireplace. The flames licked out and thawed the ice in the two pairs of hiking boots, and for the rest of the night I lay awake and felt that Deb Gardner's spirit was in the room pushing me forward. She was angry, she haunted this earth, she wanted me to do this job. That dream had propelled me for three years. The spiritual force of her untold story was bigger than any person's resistance, we were all being carried along by it. (342)

I'm not sure this was the best thing to tell the murderer. *Hey, fess up because the person you murdered wants her story told.* But it's a great thing to tell us, because it shows just how obsessed he's become, just how great the stakes are for him. As a reader, it's this kind of passage that I'm waiting for. I don't want to know how reasonable and dispassionate a reporter you are. I want to know your obsessions and your blind spots, to gauge them against my own, to make me understand and care about the human dimensions of the drama.

The Reenactment

In many ways, *Nickel and Dimed: On (Not) Getting By in America*, is a re-enactment, rather than an experiment or an infiltration. It doesn't take much effort to infiltrate the lives of the working poor by seeking a series of minimum-wage jobs. While we certainly might see such a project as a kind of social experiment, we can most likely guess the outcome. Many people turn a blind eye to the working poor of America, but it doesn't take someone with a PhD in cellular biology to determine that an hourly salary of $5.15 (minimum wage in 2001, the year *Nickel and Dimed* was published) isn't really a living wage. Okay, it *does* take some-one with a PhD in cellular biology to determine this—Ehrenreich has one. But my point is that anyone with an interest in reading her book probably won't be shocked by her findings as such. They'll be shocked on a much more human level. It's the shock of having an inkling of what the life of the person checking your groceries is like. It's not so much the findings that open our eyes as her method. By reenacting the lives of the working poor, she shows us on the ground level, rather than as a sociological study, what it means to be poor in America. It's a reenactment not of any particular life—it doesn't need to be—but of the type of life that someone who has to take two or three jobs to get by must live.

If Ehrenreich had had the idea to reenact James Agee and Walker Evans's *Let Us Now Praise Famous Men*, she might have chosen to live the life of a poor sharecropper, but the project would have gone nowhere because sharecropping was a dead institution (thankfully) by the mid-1980s. King Cotton was no longer king in the South, and the white and black farmers who had been little more than indentured servants in Agee's time, exploited as cheap labor to keep cotton viable before the universal use of machines to do their labor, were in somewhat better shape than their ancestors, but not wildly so. Many had graduated from peasant wages to being nickel and dimed. Their grandparents would have thought them rich by comparison, but in 1986 terms, they would not have thought they were living large, medium, or even junior-plus in comparison to their fellow Americans. They had simply traded in calloused hands and a hoe for a Walmart wave and a smiley-face button.

It wasn't sharecropping itself that needed reenacting, but the very chronicle of the lives of sharecroppers that James Agee and Walker Evans had made in the mid-1930s.

Fifty years after James Agee and Walker Evans traveled to Alabama, journalist Dale Maharidge and photographer Michael Williamson trekked in their footsteps to find out what had transpired in the lives of the tenant families Agee and Evans had focused on. The resulting book, *And Their Children After Them*, won the Pulitzer Prize. While definitely an investigation (and not only into the lives of the families, but into the rise and fall of the cotton economy in the South) and an infiltration, I see it also very much as a reenactment. It's nearly impossible to imagine that Maharidge and Williamson ever would have had the idea to tell the stories of these families if they hadn't had the model of Agee and Evans to follow. As soon as they drove into a small town called Centerboro, Williamson slammed on the brakes and pulled out his copy of *Let Us Now Praise Famous Men*. His memory had served him correctly: they were at the exact intersection from which Walker Evans had taken one of his famous photographs. Book in hand, they raced up and down the street until they found the exact spot from which Evans had snapped his picture half a century earlier. The photographs, reproduced side by side in the book, show a town that has remained virtually unchanged since the 1930s except for the models of the cars parked along the street.

As I've mentioned, there are degrees of immersion in any project. In some ways, any journalist deep into the research of his/her subject is an immersion journalist. Most journalists whom I've met have a certain amount of trepidation about how visible they want to be in their own book. The more traditional the journalist, the less visible she wants to be in a project, preferring to let the subject speak for itself. But, as we've discussed, no subject truly does that. Any journalist decides what to include and what to leave out, what angle to take, how to define the subject. Immersion is often a matter of degree.

As Maharidge writes of the difference between his book and Agee's:

> My effort is offered as the report of a journalist who struggled to retain his detachment. At the risk of being accused of oversimplifying the differences between the two works, I offer that I saw my proper role as standing back and observing and that Agee saw his as jumping in and experiencing. (xxii–xxiii)

But some of the most fascinating moments in the book are those in which Maharidge encounters people Agee had written about previously. Although Agee had been extraordinarily sympathetic to most of the people he encountered, he had not held back from his criticisms, and though the book sold only four hundred copies in his lifetime, Agee's words trickled back down to Alabama, as did Evans's photographs, some of them stark and upsetting to the people portrayed in them.

We'll discuss this book and Agee's further in the chapter on ethics. What I'd like to point out here is that a reenactment need not deal solely with a particular event. The reenactment of a previous chronicle and/or work of art is just as valid and potentially as fruitful. In such projects, you're using the previous work as a model, but not only that. Anyone can imaginatively or stylistically use an earlier work as a model, but the immersion writer walks in the footsteps of the writer/artist who has come before, without mimicking the prior project. If you use another work as a model in the immersion writer's sense, as a scene of reenactment, the book not only becomes about the writer's original subjects but also about the author of the original project, too. In *And Their Children After Them*, Agee certainly looms large as the troubled genius that he was. But most importantly, Maharidge makes the subject matter his own, building on the work that came before him, but not confined or cowed by it.

Before we begin such a project, we have to ask, "Why bother reenacting something in the first place?" Why does the original act need to be repeated? In the case of Maharidge, the goal is in part to see the lasting effects of cotton in the South, and more importantly (to me at least), to observe the lasting effects of a literary project upon the people observed.

Another good answer is Faulkner's famous quote about the past from *Requiem for a Nun*: "The past is never dead. It's not even past." It's true that most of us don't live in the present, or not solely in the present as, say, cats do. We're either projecting our lives forward or endlessly returning to important events from the past. Such a human tendency is writ large in the case of historical reenactors. When I lived for a time in Charlotte, North Carolina, I was always amazed by how vividly the Civil War (or "The War of Northern Aggression") still lived in the hearts and minds of many southerners, even in such a New South city as Charlotte, obsessed as it was at the time with becoming "a world class city." Every couple of months or so there would be some raging debate in the "Letters to the Editor" section of the *Charlotte Observer* about such pressing matters as who was the better general, Grant or Lee.

Tony Horwitz, in his book *Confederates in the Attic*, explores the phenomenon of Civil War reenactors after he and his wife hear a gunshot outside of their rural Virginia home one day and find a Civil War documentary being filmed in a nearby field. Before long Horwitz, himself a war correspondent, has the sleeping Civil War buff inside him awakened, and is soon traipsing around battlefields and donning Confederate gear in the company of a reenactor who specializes in playing a bloated corpse. As Roy Blount Jr. wrote in a review when the book first appeared, Horwitz "wears himself lightly" (*New York Times Sunday Book Review*, April 5, 1998) a particularly apt and revealing phrase, I think. The immersion journalist tends to wear himself or herself lightly, while the immersion memoirist doesn't. The book's aim is not to explore Horwitz's own obsession, but the obsession's meaning in the lives of others and in the culture at large. Along the way, Horwitz touches on race relations, the New South, and the various legacies of the Civil War. And he meets amazing people, from his bloated-corpse friend, Robert Lee Hodge, to the last surviving widow of a Confederate veteran who, as it turns out, was a deserter.

The Quest

In the previous chapter, we examined the quest as seen through the lens of memoir. W. Hodding Carter wanted to be the oldest competitor in the Olympics. A. J. Jacobs wanted to read the entire encyclopedia. Ammon Shea wanted to read the entire *OED*. While there are certainly universal concerns embedded in each story, the emphasis is on the self. Shea, Jacobs, and Carter are not really acting as social critics and observers so much as writers exploring their own personal obsessions.

The immersion journalist on a quest wears himself lightly, to borrow Blount's phrase, and is using his experience as a stand-in for the experience or wishes of the multitudes.

I've been holding in reserve one of the big guns of immersion journalism, but now it's time to bring him out. Please welcome George Plimpton, one of the modern pioneers of immersion journalism.

In the sixties and early seventies, Plimpton made himself into the everyman of sports, and an odd everyman he was. Here was a Harvard-educated aristocrat, classmate of Bobby Kennedy, founder and editor of the *Paris Review*, interviewer of Hemingway! What a pedigree. But he transformed himself into the hapless fan who wonders what it would be like to pitch baseball in the National League. The result was his 1961 book, *Out of My League.* These exploits were followed by his most famous book, *Paper Lion,* in which he attended the Detroit Lions training camp and participated in some scrimmages as a backup quarterback (sporting a bright blue jersey with the number *zero* on it and losing yardage in every one of his plays). Plimpton proceeded to play the fool in a variety of sports, golf, tennis, and boxing among them, always receiving a drubbing that someone else might find humiliating, but that Plimpton knew was the best outcome for his entertaining and insightful books and articles for *Sports Illustrated.*

We don't learn much about Plimpton in these books—he's not writing memoir. His goal is simply to be a stand-in for Joe Six-pack, who yells at the TV when a play goes wrong, certain he could do better than half these overpaid windbags. Of course, he knows deep in the folds of his fleshy gut that he couldn't do any better, that he'd be murdered on the field, and that's where Plimpton steps in, to offer himself up as the sacrificial goat on the altar of the average fan's unrealistic desires.

Early in the book, he asks the pro football player Raymond Berry about his chances for survival on the field. Berry advises him to play a position on the flank if he wants to survive his three-week preseason stint with the Detroit Lions. Above all, he tells the scrawny Plimpton, stay out of the "pit." The pit, he explains, is an area ten yards deep along the line of scrimmage, where all the neolithic struggles of the game are played out among three-hundred-pound linemen. But Plimpton ignores this sage advice—he *has to,* really, if you think about it. A good writer aims for conflict rather than steering clear of it. Who is the center of everyman's fear and loathing and hopeless aspirations on the field? If he's going to write an interesting book, he has to play nothing less than quarterback. So it is ordained.

We know this will be a train wreck, right? Even if he only plays in an exhibition game, he's in for some serious hurt. But what makes Plimpton an endearing everyman is that he grows on his teammates—they genuinely seem to like him and he them as the book progresses. And he takes his role quite seriously, much like a doomed Spartan soldier knowing full well he's going to come back on top of his shield rather than holding it.

What I love about Plimpton's account of the big game is how well he chronicles his feelings about himself and his role before, during, and after the game. After the huddle, he takes his position:

> My confidence was extreme. I ambled slowly behind Whitlow, poised down over the ball, and I had sufficient presence to pause, resting a hand at the base of his spine, as if on a windowsill—a nonchalant gesture I had admired in certain quarterbacks—and I looked over the length of his back to fix in my mind what I saw ... The pleasure of sport was so often the chance to indulge the cessation of time itself—the pitcher dawdling on the mound, the skier poised at the top of a mountain trail, the basketball player with the rough skin of the ball against his palm preparing for a foul shot, the tennis player at set point over his opponent—all of them savoring a moment before committing themselves to action. (23)

What Plimpton remarks at that moment seems so true that even a non-sports-lover can relish the beauty of the moment, the moment before disaster strikes, when everything still seems right, better than right, when we seem invincible, before time sweeps us up again and slams us down in its ugly fashion.

The game is a disaster for poor George. He loses yardage in every play and we feel every iota of his embarrassment and humiliation. It's our embarrassment and humiliation, too, our punishment for dreaming too big.

His teammates, feeling sorry for him, take him on a dance hall tour that evening, pounding him on the back and mimicking his patrician accent when calling for the ball: "Fawty-fowah, fawty-tew."

The next day, one of his teammates, Harley Sewell, takes him to a house where a number of Harley's friends sit in a screened-in porch, drinking coffee, and eager for details of the game the night before:

> I sat down and took some coffee. I rather looked forward to telling them. "Well, it was a disaster," I said. "Just plumb awful."

Harley was out in the kitchen overseeing something or other, the cutting of coffeecake perhaps, and he came hurrying in. He said, "Well, hold on now, I don't know about *that*."

"Come on, Harley," I said, grinning at him. "I lost nearly thirty yards in five plays . . . fell down without anyone laying a hand on me, then had the ball stolen by Roger Brown, then threw the ball ten feet over Jim Gibbons' head—that's pretty plumb awful . . ."

Harley said, "You didn't do too bad . . . *considering* . . ." He was very serious, really trying, consciously, to keep me from being upset and humiliated.

"Harley," I said, "you're a poor judge of disasters."

The others on the porch kept after me for details, but Harley wouldn't let me discuss the subject. "It don't do any good *dwelling* on such things," he said. (242)

Of course, dwelling on things is exactly what we do as writers. You can almost feel the giddiness in Plimpton's voice as he eagerly tells his audience just how "plumb awful" he was. It may have been a disaster for the part of him that yearns to be a sports hero, but for the part of him that is drawn to conflict and disaster, the writerly part, he knows he has his story. In fact, such a project offered Plimpton absolutely no chance for failure (unless he were killed!). If improbably he'd gained 99 yards for a touchdown that would have made a pretty good story, but probably not as good a story as the story of his failure. Not only is he the everyman, but he's the cheerful fool and completely self-aware of that fact. After all, his jersey is emblazoned with the number *zero*.

The Experiment

In the late 1950s, a psychologist named Milton Rokeach decided to conduct an experiment on a group of three institutionalized patients, a World War II veteran, an elderly farmer, and a failed writer, each of whom claimed to be Jesus. He wondered what would happen if he put them all together for months at a time. Would one convince the other two that they were frauds and that he was truly Jesus? That would have been interesting indeed, but it's not what happened. Each man said the other two were frauds and simply burrowed further into his self-delusion. When I first heard of this experiment—I was a teen— it sounded absurd and funny. Yes, it *is* absurd, but it's not funny. It's rather horrifying, really, and it's not something that could ever be repeated, because our notions of patients' rights, informed consent, and the like have become more enlightened. Still, Rokeach's book, *The Three Christs of Ypsilanti*, makes fascinating reading. On the face of it, Rokeach wasn't a sadist. He says he was interested in a cure; he had heard of other such encounters between similarly delusional people affecting a partial cure. But as the experiment progressed, he became more and more manipulative. When one of the men claimed to have a wife, when in fact he was a bachelor, Rokeach started writing him letters in the persona of the imaginary wife, even arranging places for them to meet. The patient would dutifully show up at these meeting spots, but of course, she would not.

Rather stunning, isn't it?

I mention this experiment to point out that the immersion writer never gets to play the Milton Rokeach role, and that's all to the good. Whether you're writing immersion memoir or immersion journalism, you don't simply get to be the observer and manipulator of others. That's not to say that manipulation is absent—artistic manipulation is a part of any good book. I stress the word *artistic*, vs. *psychological*. Psychological manipulation is not a good thing for the immersion writer to engage in, but artistic manipulation is not only a good thing, but completely necessary. By *manipulation*, I mean the ordering of events, the ways in which information is disclosed, the ways in which the writer creates tension in a narrative, and more. We're trying to bring about an effect upon the reader through the ordering of scenes, the careful divulging of information, but not by experimenting *upon* others.

Let me take that back. You do get to be Milton Rokeach, but you are simultaneously the three unfortunate patients. I can explain it this way. When I wrote my *Do-Over* book, I felt that I was in a sense three people at once (though none of them Jesus): I was the person living in the present through the various activities I had assigned myself: summer camp, kindergarten, prom. And I was in a sense the kid who had gone through these experiences in the first place. And I was the observer, the writer, the Milton Rokeach dispassionately (ha!) observing the results. The immersion writer must always be both participant and observer, but certainly never simply the observer. Naturally, such a dual (or triple) stance causes some wear and tear on the writer's psyche.

In 1959, a white journalist from Texas, John Howard Griffin, underwent skin-darkening treatments and traveled throughout the southern United States via Greyhound bus posing as an African American, at a time when race relations in the United States were about to explode, prior to the full blossoming of the civil rights movement. By today's standards, such an experiment might seem highly fraught with all sorts of cross-cultural landmines, the idea of putting on "blackness" like a suit making us (or at least me) uncomfortable. Many people would surely find the idea offensive, but it needs to be seen within the historical context of 1950s segregated South. Actually, it's a wonderful book, unpatronizing and unflinching, and reads as a fascinating time capsule and exploration of the rampant racism of that era.

But why not simply read Ralph Ellison's *Invisible Man* for a glimpse of what being a black man in white America felt like, or *Native Son*, by Richard Wright, or the essays of James Baldwin? The problem was that these books weren't high on the reading lists of white middle-class America, or if they were, they could be set aside as literary expressions to be admired and discussed at cocktail parties, and then forgotten. But a white guy pretending to be black in 1959? And aimed not at high-brow society but a middle-brow readership . . . this was a radical thing to do, an eye-opener for both Griffin and his audience. I should say, too, that I consider this book clearly an example of an immersion experiment rather than an infiltration as such. Griffin's goal was not so much to infiltrate African American culture and explain it (as though it could be monolithically explained) to white America but to experience racism in a first-hand manner and examine its pernicious effects. On the other hand, we could argue that *Black Like Me* was a kind of infiltration into Griffin's own white culture, but as a "black" man experiencing that culture.

Most importantly, Griffin presents himself as a likeable and compassionate person, more so because he decides early on in his project that he won't lie. If someone asks him who he is and what he's doing, he decides, he'll tell the truth. This happens when in New Orleans he goes to a shoeshine stand he has regularly frequented as a white man. The black proprietor, named Sterling, doesn't recognize him, but recognizes his shoes, and Griffin is forced to confess his project, which sends Sterling into fits of laughter.

"Why I'm truly a son-of-a-bitch . . . how did you ever?" Sterling asks.

Sterling agrees to coach Griffin, to allow him to hang around his shoeshine stand, though he tells Griffin right off that he's too well dressed for a "shine boy" and he needs to shave the light hairs from his hands, which Griffin attempts to do, but almost winds up making the mistake of walking into a "whites only" bathroom, a mistake he's warned away from by a group of derelicts. But Griffin doesn't have long to wait before he finds trouble, in the form of a muscular white teenager who taunts him and follows him for blocks.

"I'm going to get you, Mr. No-Hair. I'm after you. There ain't no place you go I won't get you. If it takes all night, I'll get you—so count on it."

Eventually, Griffin turns the tables on the bully, and dares him to follow him into an alley so he can use his brass knuckles on him. The bluff works and the boy disappears, though he's left Griffin terrified. As you might expect, there are plenty of lessons a white man in 1959 might learn by appearing to be African American. One of my favorite passages in the book is a scene early on in his experience, when he goes for breakfast in the Y Café and participates in a dialogue between two African Americans, one the owner of the Y Café and the other a client. The two discuss what needs to happen in the U.S. before racial equality can take hold.

> "We need a conversion of morals," the elderly man said. "Not just superficially, but profoundly. And in both races. We need a great saint—some enlightened common sense. Otherwise, we'll never have the right answers when the pressure groups—those racists, super-patriots,

whatever you want to call them—tag every move towards racial justice as communist-inspired, Zionist-inspired, Illuminati-inspired, Satan-inspired . . . part of some secret conspiracy to overthrow the Christian civilization."

"So, if you want to be a good Christian, you musn't act like one. That makes sense," Mr. Gayle said.

"That's what they claim. The minute you give me my rights to vote when I pay taxes, to have a decent job, a decent home, a decent education—then you're taking the first step toward 'race-mixing' and that's part of the great secret conspiracy to ruin civilization—to ruin America," the elderly man said.

"So if you want to be a good American, you've got to practice bad Americanism. That makes sense, too," Mr. Gayle sighed. "Maybe it'd take a saint after all to straighten such a mess out." (42–43)

Understandably, the book made a great sensation when it saw print, and Griffin received death threats by the hundreds. But it shook up much of white America in a way that it needed to be shaken up.

The Infiltration

An immersion journalist approaches infiltration in much the same manner as the immersion memoirist, but with somewhat different concerns and results. One of the cornerstones of this kind of writing is the issue of trust. Whether one is a spy or a sympathetic insider or something in between, you're not going to get very far in an infiltration if you don't earn the trust of the people you're infiltrating. This of course raises some thorny ethical issues, which we'll tackle (or at least nudge), but I'd like to wait until we get to the chapter on ethics before we do so. Simple common sense dictates that the more different you are from the group you're trying to infiltrate, the more unlikely they're going to trust your intentions from the start, as Bill Buford found in his book *Among the Thugs*, a classic of immersion journalism in which Buford chronicled the violent, disturbing world of England's soccer hooligans.

After an initial encounter with a trainload of drunken soccer fans,

Buford set out to learn more. As searches go, this was an easy one. On a train from Manchester to London in the spring of 1984, Buford went from car to car in search of a likely soccer fan he could interrogate, and found one in the form of a large beer-swilling tub of a man with a bull-dog face and a tattoo of the Red Devil, Manchester United's mascot, on his doughy bicep, and on his forearm, a Union Jack. Approaching the man, Buford explained that he was an American journalist and that he wanted to write a story on "football supporters." He wondered if the gentleman would mind a few questions?

> He stared at me. Then he said, "All Americans are wankers." And paused. "All journalists," he added, showing, perhaps, that his mind did not work along strictly nationalist lines, "are cunts."
> We had established a rapport. (26)

Indeed, they had. Despite the man's bluster, he seemed more than happy to talk to an American journalist. Buford, expecting all foot-ball fans to fit into his stereotype of unemployed and disenfranchised young men, found in Mick (as the man introduced himself) a relatively happy, if vulgar, well-employed electrician with a decent income. Given the chance, most people want to chat about their obsessions, and this goes double for sports fans. Mick was no exception. By the end of their encounter, Buford found that Mick was "open and generous and trust-ing. That was the thing: He trusted me."

Kevin Roose, another spy in the Buford mold, had the idea to trans-fer for a semester from liberal, Ivy-league Brown University to the bedrock conservative Christian school Liberty University, founded by the Reverend Jerry Falwell in Lynchburg, Virginia. Roose, a protégé of and one-time assistant to A. J. Jacobs, was first introduced to the world of born-again Christianity when he accompanied Jacobs to Falwell's twenty-thousand-member megachurch, Thomas Road Baptist Church, while conducting research for Jacobs's *The Year of Living Biblically*. Roose had grown up in liberal Oberlin, Ohio, the son of nonobservant, politically active Quaker parents (on the other side of the political spec-trum from Falwell). After an awkward conversation in the lobby of the church with a group of Liberty students, he spent some time on the

Internet researching conservative Christianity and hatched the idea to do a kind of American version of a semester study abroad by enrolling for a semester at Liberty University. After getting permission from the surprised dean of students at Brown and his reluctant parents, Roose set some ground rules for himself.

An immersion project can succeed or fail on the basis of the writer's attitude toward his subject, and the subsequent tone he takes in writing about it. Wisely, Roose chooses not to go into his project, *The Unlikely Disciple*, with the intent of mocking born-agains, which P. J. O'Rourke once likened to "hunting dairy cows with a high-powered rifle and scope" (Roose, 11). In order for the project to work, Roose feels he needs to approach it with an open mind and as honestly as possible . . . to a point:

> Naturally, I wanted to be as honest as possible. I wasn't eager to sneak around like a spy, and I didn't want the mental burden of juggling a double identity, so I decided to stick to my guns: regular old Kevin Roose from Oberlin, Ohio. No alias, no faked documents, no lies about my past. If people asked, I'd tell them that I came to Liberty from Brown, and if they asked why, I'd say, "I wanted to see what Christian college was like." (11)

Comfortable with the fact or not, he *is* a spy, but a sympathetic spy. Under certain conditions, he knows he'll have to be evasive. In filling out the admissions essay online, he first culls some born-again jargon from various Web sites and cobbles it together. Then his one conservative Christian friend gives him a three-day crash course in Christian dogma. Most importantly, he plans not to tell anyone at Liberty he's going to write about his experiences. When they pray, he'll pray. When they sing hymns, he'll sing hymns. Is there a possibility he might convert? An outside chance, he acknowledges, but it's unlikely. While he's sympathetic to the friends he makes at Liberty, admirably refusing to stereotype or pigeonhole them, it's unlikely that one semester's immersion at Liberty will make him eschew his beliefs in regard to homosexuality and other hot-button issues that divide the left and the right in the U.S. He's there to gather information, and gather he does, with a surprising amount of insight and maturity for one so young. Some people will and do find such a project offensive, as the many comments on the Amazon Web site illustrate, but a number of people in the conservative Christian community think otherwise, believing that the book should be required reading at Liberty. An outsider can often give you a better view of your strengths and weaknesses than an insider can.

As Roose learns in his project, a spy's life is not an easy one. As his project continues, he finds himself more and more emotionally invested in the people he meets, worried about the reactions of his friends when they find out he's been lying to them, concerned about the ramifications of dating Anna, one of his classmates at Liberty, and becoming increasingly distressed by the gay-bashing he encounters among his friends.

Not all spies get caught in their own schemes and machinations, but all are in some ways implicated. As an immersion journalist, it's often impossible to stay above the fray. That's not to say that you necessarily will suffer a mental or spiritual collapse, but you'll likely encounter some version of a dark night of the soul.

The agenda of a spy and the agenda of a sympathetic insider are not all that different from one another, though it may seem otherwise on the face of it. If you're writing about someone and you have inside knowledge of them, you're unmasking them in one way or another for potentially thousands of readers. They don't always like that, regardless of your intentions. Of course, in the case of a group of people such as the Amish, who are widely stereotyped, that unmasking might not be a bad thing—if you do it right.

In *Plain Secrets: An Outsider Among the Amish*, Joe Mackall does just that. Living in Ohio, surrounded, as it were, by forty thousand Amish, "the largest Amish settlement in the world," Mackall becomes an insider gradually. First he approaches his neighbor Samuel, a thirty-seven-year-old farmer from the Schwartzentruber denomination, to ask if he can board his daughter's horse. Samuel is hesitant at first, but agrees after asking Mackall to sign a contract saying Mackall won't sue if anything happens to the horse while under Samuel's care. He's heard (he admits later) that the "English," as outsiders are called, sue each other over anything and everything. Six months later, the trust between the two men develops further when Mackall offers to drive Samuel to his mother's funeral in Ontario, Canada. It's no small offer: Mackall lives in Ohio and the drive takes the better part of a night. When they arrive at Samuel's parents' home, Mackall is still the outsider; rather than follow Samuel inside, he stays alone in his car, though later he's invited inside the house of Samuel's brother, where he spends "the coldest hours of my life."

Chance meetings and curiosity are often what bring us into the lives of other people. Mackall started with little interest in the Amish, and less knowledge. One of the first things he divulges is that he stereotyped them as most of us do. He saw them as a monolithic culture. When he spoke of the Amish, he spoke of them as a unified group, all of whom reject cars and other modern comforts. In fact, *the Amish* is about as accurate a term as lumping all the various indigenous tribes in America together and labeling them *Indians* or *Native Americans*. He learns first of all that there are many different types of denominations of Amish, and that his neighbor belongs to the most conservative of these, the Schwartzentrubers. The Schwartzentrubers are such a conservative order that they won't even place "slow vehicle" warning signs on their buggies, and other Amish groups make fun of them for milking cows by hand, calling them "*gruddel vullahs*," wooly lumps, for the milk that gets caught in their beards.

Mackall's infiltration is a slow process, taking him twelve years to gain their trust, though he says he wanted to write a book about them from the outset. He admits that he's not even sure why his neighbor eventually gives him his consent and unprecedented access by an outsider to their way of life—which Mackall takes pains to avoid romanticizing. There are plenty of things he admires about his neighbors' way of life, but other things he finds repellant, such as their treatment of women—girls stop going to school after eighth grade and are bred to breed.

It's easy for a reader to see why Samuel allows Mackall such an insider's look. It's no fluke that Mackall drove on his own initiative and presumably his own expense to Canada so his neighbor could attend his mother's funeral. Throughout the book, Mackall comes across as honest and compassionate, and after twelve years of living in close proximity, it's clear that their relationship is not a one-way infiltration. As Mackall tells it:

> Members of the Shetler family have become our friends, not just our "Amish friends." They have reinforced what I hope I'll never forget, which is that to have any real chance of knowing anything about people different from yourself, you must get to know the individuals of that social group, or race, or nationality. Nothing less will do. In our case, it is this family. We have cried with them, laughed with them, worried with them and for them, shaken our heads in dismay at their behavior, and shaken our heads just as hard at our own.
>
> I have gained access to this family because the Shetler family and mine have gone through much together. We were there when several of their children were born, and we were with them when their oldest child died. She was nine. We have eaten dinner at their house and sought refuge with them when an ice storm cut off our electricity for three days. We've been there when an insurance company planned to seize their farm and when the county authorities threatened to throw Samuel and several of his Amish neighbors in jail. (xxix–xxx)

While we see Samuel and his family through Mackall's eyes, and Mackall is not shy to include himself in various scenes and comment on events, the focus is always clearly on his subjects, not himself. He's simply there as a kind of filter, interpreter, and advocate.

Rebecca Skloot began an investigation that turned into an infiltration when she was a sixteen-year-old community college student. Taking a biology class to satisfy a requirement, her interest was piqued when her instructor told the class about HeLa cells. These cells were harvested from a biopsy done without the permission or knowledge of a terminally ill African American woman in 1951, and became the first "immortal cells" ever to be successfully reproduced in a lab. The cancer cells of Henrietta Lacks have since been used in the polio vaccine, chemotherapy, cloning, have been shot into space, have been reproduced in laboratories around the world by the trillions, and if all the HeLa cells ever cultured were amassed somehow, they'd weigh an estimated fifty metric tons. Millions of dollars have been made as a result of this woman's unwitting contribution, though her family never saw a dime and didn't even know, until recently, about the uses to which Lacks's cells had been put for many years.

But Skloot didn't know all that when she first took that biology class in 1988. She was simply curious and her curiosity led her to ask three questions of her instructor after class, when she followed him to his office. "Where was she from . . . ? Did she know how important her cells were? Did she have any children?" (4).

Her instructor didn't know. And that set her on her investigation, slowly, and like many of the best investigations, she didn't really know it was an investigation or that it would be a book until years later. At first, Skloot was curious. Then she became obsessed. Then she had a book, *The Immortal Life of Henrietta Lacks*, which took her all of ten years to complete and brought her places she had no idea about when she first asked those three simple questions.

That's the thing about any such immersion project. You don't know what you'll find or how it will change you, and immersion projects almost invariably do change you. The artist Milton Avery said that art was a series of blind corners, and it's much the same with anything that you approach with your mind open.

Skloot allows us to experience the various blind corners along with her—first, she had to gain the trust of Henrietta's suspicious family, especially Henrietta's daughter, Deborah. Why should they trust a young white girl, another curiosity seeker aiming to exploit them? Happily, Skloot was able to slip through their defenses through her own dogged persistence and her obvious generosity of spirit. The story she wanted to tell from the beginning was not a purely scientific one, but rather a biography of an American family. You can see this from the questions she first asked her teacher when she was sixteen. They're all focused on the people involved, not on the science itself. "Where was she from . . . ? Did she know how important her cells were? Did she have any children?" While there's plenty about the scientific uses of HeLa cells in the book, Skloot's concerns remain squarely with Henrietta's family. Without the story of Skloot's successful infiltration into the Lacks family, the book would merely be an investigative report, a kind of scientific anecdote: gee, did you know that these miraculous cells came from the same woman? Look at all that's been done with them to help humanity! Such a report might have made for a good article in a popular science journal, but what makes the book so compelling is that Skloot shows us the human side of the science by slowly gaining the trust of and becoming close to the family.

Skloot weaves together the history of the HeLa cell, the history of Henrietta and the Lacks clan, and the story of trying to find that story. So there are three narratives threading their way through the story. In the chapters in which the writer's experience is not necessary—Henrietta's story, the story of the scientists involved with the research, the story of what happened to Henrietta's children after she died—Skloot absents herself entirely. By doing this, she allows the story its own force and dignity. An intrusion of Skloot into the chapters in which she tells the stories of Henrietta's family and the story of her cells would certainly have seemed self-indulgent and unprofessional. But her story of getting the story, of slowly winning the confidence and trust of the Lacks family, and especially of Henrietta's daughter, Deborah, is every bit as gripping and relevant as the other two strands. Take this scene, for instance, in which Skloot, frustrated that no one will talk to her, drives to the small, impoverished community in which Henrietta lived, Turner Station. Armed only with her own determination and an old newspaper article, Skloot goes in search of a local grocery store in which the article reported the owner, a woman named Courtney Speed, had erected a little memorial and wanted to create a museum for Henrietta. Skloot has an address, but all she sees when she gets there is an old trailer with some people sitting on the steps. It doesn't look like a store and she keeps driving around it, arousing the curiosity of nearly everyone in the town, it seems, all of them black, who wave at her every time she passes as though noticing her for the first time. Finally, she meets a pastor who obligingly leads her right back to the trailer, which turns out to be the very same grocery store for which she was searching. Here she meets Courtney Speed, who is friendly and solicitous until Rebecca mentions the purpose of her visit:

Courtney gasped, her face suddenly ashen. She took several steps backwards and hissed, "You know Mr. Cofield? Did he send you?"

I was confused. I told her I'd never heard of Cofield, and no one had
sent me.

"How did you know about me?" she snapped, backing away further.

I pulled the old crumpled newspaper article from my purse and
handed it to her.

"Have you talked to the family?" she asked.

"I'm trying," I said. "I talked to Deborah once, and I was supposed to
meet Sonny today, but he didn't show up."

She nodded, like I *knew* it. "I can't tell you anything until you got the
support of the family. I can't risk that." (72–73)

A number of my students worry about how much of themselves they
should include in a story that is essentially not about them. They often
shy away from the very thing that will make a book work—the human
dimension—and we wind up with a kind of disembodied narration
guiding us through another person's life as though through the rooms
of a dusty and forgotten museum. I fail to see how that makes a book
somehow more artful, more professional, or less self-indulgent. To me,
it's an act of generosity to the reader to introduce yourself, to say, *This
is who I am and why this story is important to me, and these are the people
I met along the way.*

Another infiltrator is the writer Norah Vincent, who in *Self-Made
Man: One Woman's Journey into Manhood and Back*, takes on, in *Black
Like Me* fashion, a male identity, and participates in various stereotypical male activities: going to strip clubs, joining a bowling league, going
on a men's retreat, even working and dating as a man. She's not doing
this to write an exposé as such, but to deeply examine the cultural and
emotional divides that separate men and women. When she transforms
into a male, she calls herself Ned. She's a spy in the fullest sense of the
word, and yet she finds herself in sympathy with Americans males,
with the heaviness of the mantle of manhood, by the end of her project
(strikingly, the project lasts eighteen months, breaking the mold of the
typical year-long immersion project). But like many others, she finds

the emotional price of infiltration much more taxing than she imagined at the outset:

> I had to do a lot of crossing out when I crossed from woman to man. I hadn't anticipated this when I'd started as Ned. I had thought that by being a guy I would get to do all the things I didn't get to do as a woman, things I'd always envied about boyhood when I was a child: the perceived freedoms of being unafraid in the world, stamping around loudly with my legs apart. But when it actually came to the business of being Ned I rarely felt free at all ... I couldn't be myself, and after a while, this really got me down. (275–76)

So down, in fact, that one night she wound up in a semicatatonic state in her pajamas at a hospital, signing herself into a psych ward. Such are the hazards of immersion writing. One thing's for certain: the book you set out to write and the book you end up with are usually far apart, and you might not have agreed to write your project had you possessed the knowledge going in to the project that you possess after you emerge on the other end. "[A] lot can change between the proposal and the finished book," Vincent writes, "and always does. That is the whole purpose, after all. If you knew what was going to happen in the end, there would be no point in starting. Setting out to prove a point only colors the experience and then skews the results more than your inescapable subjectivity and prejudices already do. You have to leap. You have to be a bit reckless. Maybe more than a bit. Maybe a lot" (3–4).

Infiltration projects should carry internal labels: *Warning, this project might be hazardous to your psyche.*

Vincent's is a book of immersion journalism that led to a book of immersion memoir. In *Self-Made Man*, she's examining what it means to be male. The goal isn't to peel away layers of self, even if that inadvertently is what happens. Remember that passage in Nellie Bly's work that I was so fascinated by, when after a harrowing night of recounting her life, bit by bit, she comes face to face with self? In Bly's case, she leaves this confrontation to the reader's imagination, as this was the convention of the time. In Vincent's case, she shows us that self laid bare in her follow-up memoir, *Voluntary Madness: My Year Lost and Found in the Loony Bin,* in which she, like Nellie Bly, checks herself into three psychiatric wards to investigate the disparities in treatment at various institutions, public and private.

What fascinates me about this book in part is how Vincent first envisioned it, she says, as a piece of immersion journalism—definitely in the Nellie Bly vein, but how, as the project progressed, the exploration became more and more intensely personal. How could it help being so? The spy is very much an actor, the kind of actor who will do anything to inhabit his/her role. We've all read of actors who have taken training too far, gaining or losing absurd amounts of weight, often at the price of health and mental well-being. In a similar fashion, Vincent stopped her antidepressant medication in order to lapse back into depression, and subsequently checked herself into a private hospital. A writer who is going to do such a thing runs the same risks as the actor who merges dangerously with the role she's playing. Vincent writes in her introduction:

> As you read, you will see that what begins as the mostly detached report of the proverbial journalist at large . . . and then merges indistinguishably with the very personal account of a bona fide patient's search for rescue and, if possible, a touch of lasting self-awareness along the way. (10)

Immersion isn't for the faint of heart. Whether you're putting yourself in harm's way emotionally, psychologically, or physically, it's almost a guarantee that you're going to get pummeled in one way or another.

Exercises

1. You might think that Horwitz, with his Civil War reenactment, has claimed for himself the best reenactment story possible, and it's true that his is a hard act to top, but there's not just one group of reenactors in the world to write about. What about African American Civil War reenactors? Or medieval reenactors? Or the Japanese couples who visit Nova Scotia for *Anne-of-Green-Gables*-themed weddings . . . there are

dozens, probably hundreds of reenactments ripe for writing about, and not every type of reenactment is a reenactment of something military or even something that actually happened. Do a little research on the subject and spend a weekend with some reenactors in your vicinity (defining reenactment as loosely as you like). Join in if you can and try to understand their obsession. Has it been communicated to you so well that it's now your obsession, too?

2. Write your own version of a tongue-in-cheek "black like me" or "self-made man" experiment. Perhaps go undercover in the chess club. "Chess Club Like Me." Or become a volunteer for a rival political party and pretend to be a rabid fill-in-the-blank.

3. Become an everyman/everywoman. Identify an experience à la Barbara Ehrenreich or George Plimpton, in which you are taking on a role either well above your abilities or well below. Try to focus the experience so that its goal is to say something about the society in which you live, rather than only your own goals and aspirations.

4. Volunteer in your community. Work at a nursing home, read to disadvantaged children, put in a shift at the local soup kitchen—take yourself away from your normal comfort zone and do something for someone else. Keep a journal of your time volunteering. You might get an essay from the experience, but even if it's only a prose blob, you're engaging with the world and your community in a way that will enrich your subject matter—and you'll be doing a good deed.

5. Imagine yourself a contemporary Nellie Bly. If you were to do an exposé, what would you try to infiltrate and why? Has anyone else done such an infiltration?

Chapter Three

Travel Writing

Here's a bold assertion: I'd like to claim Herodotus, the so-called Father of History, as the first immersion writer. The first travel writer, too, he was no armchair traveler, but a true globetrotter of the ancient world, roving far and wide in the fifth century BCE to collect stories of the various peoples of the known world. While little is known of his life, his reports on the cultures of the ancient world shimmer with his personality, with his opinions and beliefs, likes and dislikes. He doesn't pretend to be objective but says, *This is what I heard. This is what people have told me.* In Arabia, for instance, he describes the landscape, the people, and their customs, invariably telling us what he's observed firsthand, and what is mere hearsay. Take a look at the following passage (a report on flying snakes!) and you'll see what I mean:

> There is a place in Arabia more or less opposite the city of Buto, where I went to try to get information about the flying snakes. On my arrival I saw their skeletons in incalculable numbers; they were piled in heaps, some of which were big, others smaller, others smaller still, and there were many piles of them. The place where these bones lie is a narrow mountain pass leading to a broad plain which joins on to the plain of Egypt, and it is said that when the winged snakes fly to Egypt from Arabia in spring, the ibises meet them at the entrance to the pass and do not let them get through, but kill them. According to the Arabians, this service is the reason for the great reverence with which the ibis is re-

garded in Egypt, and the Egyptians themselves admit the truth of what
they say. (124)

This is what makes his writing so engaging—we're engaged precisely
because he admits his subjectivity. We tend to believe someone more
readily when they say, *I saw this with my own eyes*. But flying snakes?
What an image. I'd like to think that flying snakes never existed. I don't
know what exactly he saw, but I'm willing to believe he saw something
that he was told were the skeletons of flying snakes. He says, "On my
arrival, I saw their skeletons in incalculable numbers . . ." There's an implied scene here; we can almost imagine ourselves arriving in the city of
Buto on a blistering day, a couple of slaves taking our bags through the
crowded streets of the market, and then when we arrive at our lodgings
(the Ibis Hotel, of course), the proprietor offers to arrange a tour of the
Plain of Egypt where we'll see, among other wonders, flying snakes.
And it will only set us back fifty Athenian owls. Such a deal! He ne-
glects to tell us the flying snakes are snake skeletons, but hey, the term
caveat emptor, or *buyer beware*, is a Roman term and so hasn't been invented yet. So then how about . . . live and learn? Maybe that's a Greek
truism.

It's so much easier for us to identify with a person who lives and
breathes, or once did, then it is for us to understand disembodied information delivered impersonally in encyclopedic fashion:

> Some ancient observers claimed that winged snakes migrated annu-
> ally from the Arabian peninsula to the Egyptian Plains but were feasted
> upon by waiting Ibis. Sometimes depicted in Egyptian funerary art,
> winged snakes might have been an exaggeration of sand vipers, which
> throw themselves at their victims, or the partially shed skin of a snake,
> which might resemble wings, or perhaps even the hood of a cobra.

Which would you rather read? Personally, I'd go for Herodotus precisely because he is so personable. The other information intrigues,
but it's no more objective than Herodotus's account. Note that it's rife
with speculation and equivocation, but it aspires to a kind of authori-
tative tone without really meriting it. In that way, I'd say the firsthand

account, if not more accurate, is at least more honest. It invites doubt and skepticism, neither of which are bad attributes when approaching any written text, even this. You should always be prepared to argue with a good book.

Of all forms of immersion writing, travel writing is the most venerable and has had the most practitioners. Who wouldn't want to be a travel writer? It sounds on the face of it like a lark. You get to stay in fancy hotels, travel, and eat on an expense account. Well, sort of. If you're a celebrity author and *Travel and Leisure* rings and says, "Damon, we're in need of someone to do a piece for us on the world's only eight-star hotel, which is constructed entirely of endangered coral. It's off the coast of Malaysia, accessible only by amphibious landing craft. Just 750 words should do it. Would you be a love and head there next weekend? I'll ask Dagmar to swing by with the corporate jet to take you as far as Kuala Lumpur."

We wish. The realities of travel writing are far less glamorous, but there's plenty of adventure to be had, and if you're willing to write *on spec* (short for *on speculation*, not as an assigned piece of writing, meaning there's no guarantee you'll be published or paid), there's little to stop you. There are so many possible outlets for your travel pieces, from a privately produced travel blog to writing pieces for print magazines and well-established online travel magazines such as *World Hum*. As in journalism, there's almost always *some* immersion involved in travel writing, but for it to truly be a piece of immersion writing, it has to include the narrator and not simply be standard guidebook fare listing the best places to eat and stay the night. That's not to disparage guidebook writing or writers. The well-known travel writer Pico Iyer got his start gallivanting around Europe on a shoestring writing guidebook copy. And a good friend in Iowa City, where I live, writes Lonely Planet guides for the southwestern U.S. and Disneyworld, and enjoys her work. But a guidebook doesn't leave a lot of leeway for the writer's personality—it's meant essentially to provide information first, entertainment second. The problem with such writing is that the advances that authors receive to write their guidebooks are relatively small, and if you're not great at budgeting, you might find yourself with a looming deadline, empty wallet, and a lot of ground to cover yet, as Thomas Kohnstamm found in his controversial romp, *Do Travel Writers Go to Hell?* In the book, he exposes travel writing's tawdry side—succumbing to the temptation to sometimes rely on second-hand information and accept freebies from local businesses (a strict no-no for guidebook writers, whose words means dollars to these businesses). These revelations don't surprise me *that* much. The first time I visited the Philippines in 1999, Lonely Planet guide in hand, I remember arriving at one empty lot after another purported to have the best Lumpiang Shanghai in town or a cheap place to sleep. That's not to say that all guidebook writers take such shortcuts. I'd trust my friend Jennifer's recommendation to ride "The Tower of Terror" versus the "It's a Small World After All" ride any day. But the point is that travel writers of this kind aren't paid to be creative.

No one's going to give you any kind of budget for the creative kind of travel essay unless you have a track record. For the writer starting out, you always have to write the piece on spec and then see if anyone wants to publish it, and then you have to amass a number of examples of your work to show editors, called a *clip file*. While there are plenty of online travel sites at which to try your hand, many are every bit as selective as print journals, and so it might be worthwhile starting off with a travel blog. It's not always simple to develop an audience, but if you're a traveler to begin with and your writing is insightful, entertaining, witty, or any combination thereof, you can start to develop an audience *and* use your blog as a stepping stone to other venues, both online and in print. Regardless of the end results, the value of a travel blog is in the blog itself, since even if you only have an audience of five, you still have a record of your travels.

In my own case, when I traveled with my family for a year to the Philippines not long ago, I queried an editor at *McSweeney's Internet Tendency*, the online version of the well-known journal, to see if they might like for me to write a series of dispatches for them while I was abroad. The editor was happy to consider this, but he wanted to see a sample. Now I should pause here and state that this was a nonpaying gig, and while I often get paid for my work, that's not always the case. You have to weigh the benefits, and I thought the benefits of writing a piece for a prestigious Internet site that's read by thousands outweighed the fact that my column wouldn't even buy me a cup of coffee. Such is the writer's life, and while you want to be judicious, writing for free doesn't mean that it's worthless.

I wrote my first column not long after landing in Manila, and I tried as deftly as possible not only to tell a story that would entertain and inform, but also to give the reader necessary context, the basics. Who is telling this story and why is he here? And who are all these other people around him? I often find that this is the first thing that's missing from many such pieces—if we don't know who you are, why should we follow you? Of course, *you* know who you are, and so you might naturally think that the basics of your life are boring and unnecessary, but that's a somewhat lazy attitude. The reader needs this basic information, and there are ways to give it to the reader without it seeming as though you're reciting your driver's license. Here's an example from "Dispatches from Manila":

Daisy's Debut

Margie and I have barely touched down in the Philippines when I learn that I'm to attend the "debut" of Daisy, the daughter of my wife's first cousin Peach and Peach's husband, the inimitable Bong Bong. After 19 hours of flying from the States—well, under any circumstances— Daisy's debut wouldn't make my personal Lonely Planet index of must-do's in Manila. File this under family obligation. Peach and Margie are practically sisters.

John Cheever spent his Guggenheim year in Italy. I've chosen the Philippines, which seems fitting: for a somewhat more down-market writer to live in a somewhat more down-market country. I love Italy, too, but nothing's quite like the Philippines. My wife is from here, and I've come here so often since 1998, when I started researching a book set in the Philippines, that I've come to feel at home in this bedraggled and ever-surprising archipelago of 7,107 islands (at low tide, as the joke goes).

The debut is to be held at Peach and Bong Bong's restaurant, Titanic. Restaurant? Since when do Peach and Bong Bong have a restaurant, I want to know, as I'm peeling myself out of my sweaty travel clothes and indulging in a little pre-debut whining. What happened to their medical laboratory?

"*Cerrado*," Margie tells me with a shrug and a schadenfreude smile. It failed. Over the eight years I've been a part of this family, Peach and Bong Bong have had at least three business ventures that I know of: the medical laboratory, another restaurant, and buying and reselling cars. The simple reason that they can afford to hop from one failed business to another is Bong Bong's mother, who lives and works in the U.S. and sends them money. Bong Bong's mother petitioned for him to join her in the States, but he couldn't wait and went there about nine years ago using a fake passport, was caught, and deported. While he was there, he made pretty good money, working three jobs, but he wept every night on the phone talking to his kids. He probably wouldn't have been caught if he hadn't returned to the Philippines on a visit.

I love all of Margie's relatives, even, or maybe especially, the nutty ones, being a little nutty myself. Titanic! Indeed. How did they ever come up with a name like that? "The kids suggested it," Margie tells me. "They all loved the movie." With that same smile, she gives me this: "Peach told Merle [Margie's older sister], 'I don't know where I got my business sense.'" A gale of laughter overcomes us and my jet lag has been temporarily relieved.

Still, in the car on the way to Titanic, I wonder if perhaps Italy would have been the better choice. No one would force me to attend a debut, at least not this kind of debut, the Filipino version of a debutante's coming out. An opera debut, maybe. Do they still write operas in Italy? Who's the contemporary Puccini? If only I wrote about Westchester County! I'm lost in this Italian/John Cheever daydream as we crawl through Manila's legendary traffic.

We're the first guests to arrive at Titanic. The restaurant is tucked into a dreary corner on a busy but not interesting street. The restaurant has been open a year already, but no one seems to want to visit a restaurant named Titanic, for some reason. The sign doesn't help. It depicts a singing chef on the deck of a sinking ocean liner. Nor has the frequent turnover in staff or the frequent turnover of the menu helped. What cuisine does a sinking ocean liner serve? Seven months ago, it was French. Three months ago, it was Italian. Now it's Filipino.

The restaurant's interior likewise reflects its owners' indecision/desperation. Posters on the wall advertise "General Chicken," "Lechon Kawali," and "Bouillabaisse." Tonight, the interior is also decorated to the nines with balloons and banners, a strobe light and a gay comedian. I say "decorated" with a gay comedian because gay comedians are a kind of decoration in this country. And when I say "gay" I mean "effeminate," because that's about the only acceptable gay persona in the Philippines. The TV shows are peppered liberally, or not so liberally (considering the dominance of the Catholic Church), with effeminate gay men, known here derisively as *bakla*. I've never quite known how to process the Philippines' obsession with effeminate gay men. An ex-pat British poet I once met thought it had something to do with the macho norm of Filipino men, a kind of safety valve for the other extreme in male representation. I don't know, but I find alternately fascinating and discomfiting the sheer uniformity of gay representation.

This particular performer wears a kind of mod cap and has blond hair extensions. As people start to trickle in and take the seats, he sets up the karaoke machine, tests the fog machine, and glances at me curiously. Of course, I'm going to be the only white person at the debut tonight, unless you count Peach, who regularly injects herself with whitening solution. (Filipinos are as enamored of whiteness as white Americans are enamored of tanning.)

The show gets started when Daisy and her parents show up—Bong Bong breezes by me with a cursory "Wazzup?," though ghostly white Peach and I exchange pleasantries.

You'd never know by looking at Peach that she has seven children. In typical Filipina fashion, Peach looks about 15 rather than her actual age of 39.

I congratulate her on the success of her restaurant and the loveliness of her daughters. At least the latter comment isn't insincere. Daisy, in her yellow gown, looks more elegant and sophisticated than most

18-year-olds. And Daisy's older sister Cheska, well, she's the family star.
She was the runner-up for Miss Philippines this year, and that counts for
a lot in this beauty-pageant-obsessed country.

The comedian is also a singer, starting with a rousing version of "Bo-
hemian Rhapsody" while TV images that have no connection to the
music flash on the screen behind him. Obese Polynesian dancers shake
their grass-skirted booties while our host sings, "Mama, I just killed
a man!"

The moment I've been dreading arrives when he stops singing and
starts going through the crowd. I freeze. Maybe if I close my eyes I'll
become invisible. It worked when I was 2. The audience is made up
largely of teens, who seem to find nothing about the comedian amusing
or even worth paying attention to.

"What do you wish for Daisy on her birthday?" he asks them in turn.
Several say the exact same thing: "Well, I just met Daisy tonight, so I
don't really know her. But I wish her all the best."

As I'm critiquing their insincere wishes and trying desperately to
concoct my own insincere wishes, the comic approaches me.

"Are you afraid of me?" he asks.

"Terribly," I say.

"You don't have to be afraid," he says. "I'm good. What do you
wish?"

Besides my wish to be in Italy right now, I can't think of a thing.

"I wish her all the best," I say.

Spurred on by my originality and warmth toward the birthday girl,
no doubt, Margie wishes what's-her-name "good luck in life and good
health." Here, here! Can we go home now? But then, in a surprise move
that touches even my alabaster heart, young Daisy stops by the table and
gives me a rose. "Thank you," I say, though in an instant I discern this is
not an ordinary rose.

"Why did she give me a rose?" I ask Margie.

"She gives roses to 18 boys," Margie says, air-quoting heavily the word
"boys." "Each one takes a turn dancing with her."

"Come on, Daisy," the comic says, suddenly as impatient as me, it
seems, to get this over with. "Form your line."

Daisy looks over the lot of us, who are as eager as slave laborers, and bursts into tears. The comic stands behind her, his shoulders shaking, his face collapsing in mock sentiment. He dabs his eyes with a handkerchief and sticks it up his nose. On the stereo, Frank Sinatra sings "The Way You Look Tonight" to Daisy as though he's never sung it to anyone else, and before I know it it's my turn.

When I'm up there, you know, dancing with an 18-year-old as manufactured fog rolls thickly around me, having surrendered to the futility of it all—youth, dignity, presence of mind—I can almost fool myself into believing that I don't look half bad, that I might be starting to enjoy myself, that this place might have something over Italy after all. But then my 5-year-old rushes the stage after my performance and says breathlessly, "Dad, promise me you'll never do that again."

"Why?" I ask, laughing.

"You know!" she says, and leaves it at that, but really I don't. How could I know? I can't even read my own mind. "*Bahala na,*" I tell her over the music, the Filipino version of *Que será, será.* Sincerely. (*McSweeney's Internet Tendency,* November 7, 2008)

When I first wrote that, I didn't know how it would be received, especially by Filipino communities both inside the Philippines and abroad. One difference between writing about other cultures now as opposed to fifty years ago is that you cannot assume that your audience all look and act like you and come from the same background. In the past, travel writers might patronize and condescend towards other cultures and few would be bothered. But in our ever more intimately connected world, you can bet that people you think of as cute, weird, or exotic won't find your generalizations so charming. While you're looking at the Other (a term that always puts me in mind of some kind of matinee movie monster: *Attack of The Other!*) the Other is looking at you. The best you can do is have more than a passing knowledge about the culture in which you find yourself, read what others have written, and look beyond your first impressions. Even so, I sometimes run across observations about other cultures that make me cringe. Occasionally, I'll still read some sentimental portrait of another culture in which the writer makes a statement to the effect of: "The warm smiles and laughter of these gentle forest people as they cavorted in the stream made me forget the March of Time and the stresses of my normally hectic life." Maybe people are as uncomplicated and exotic as that in a theme park, but such generalizations only highlight your own naïveté, and say nothing about the people of whom you're a casual observer. Rule of thumb: stay clear of any travel writer who writes about natives cavorting. That's not to say that as an outsider your observations are of little value. On the contrary, it can be fascinating for a cultural insider to see how a relatively informed insider views their culture. I found this out after the first one or two pieces I wrote on the Philippines, when, to my great relief, I started receiving positive emails from Filipinos who, thanks to the accessibility of the Internet, were able to read my columns around the world.

In the days of the old empires, the travel writer made forays into the far reaches of the colonies and brought back tales of eccentric, exotic, and amusing natives and their weird practices. Now, more often than not, the traveler is exploring his or her own eccentricities and odd behaviors—travel is a great prism through which to view the self. That's one reason I travel—to see myself and my own culture in sharper relief against unfamiliar landscapes. As you'll notice in the example above, the piece is as much (if not more) about me than it is about the Philippines, though hopefully, a reader can garner some insights into Filipino culture by reading the column. What's important is that I'm not passing judgment and I'm not approaching the Philippines with feelings of my own culture's supremacy. Nor am I romanticizing Filipino culture and saying what happy, carefree people they are in their restaurant habitat.

Not a blog, but a radio podcast, *The Global Guru* (http://www .prx.org/series/31539-global-guru-radio) is the brainchild of travel writer Rachel Louise Snyder, who visits different locales around the world to explore one quirky cultural question at a time, such as how to dance away spider bites in Sicily, how to negotiate land disputes in East Timor, how did Tanzania become the capitol of barbershops, and how do Cambodians predict the harvest each year? What's particularly smart about Snyder's broadcasts is that she purposefully resists stereotypical associations Americans might have with such countries as Afghanistan, Thailand, and Rwanda. As she demonstrates, the best travelers are the most curious, those who don't view difference as an obstacle but as an opportunity to ask another question.

Immersion of any kind is not for the casual hobbyist. If you're going to engage in travel writing, as with any other form of immersion, you must immerse yourself completely and somewhat obsessively. There are few shortcuts, and if you're interested in travel, why would you want to take a shortcut, anyway? The long way around is typically the most interesting. As Saint Augustine wrote, "The world is a book, and those who do not travel read only a page." I must add one caveat to the discussion that follows. The number of fine travel books that have been written is vast, and I can't hope to touch on them all, nor would I want to do so. This book is intended as a writing guide first and an extended meditation on various examples of the forms second. Instead of focusing on travel classics written by Twain, Steinbeck, Paul Theroux, Bruce Chatwin, V. S. Naipaul, et al., my examples will be slightly less canonical, in part to introduce you to worthy writers you might not ordinarily encounter, and in part simply because the examples I've chosen are ones that leapt first to my mind and illustrate my points best, or that at least is my hope.

The Infiltration

In some ways, all travelers are infiltrators. The tourist is of course the least successful of infiltrators, willing to see only the shiny surface of a far-off country and say he's been there, wherever that is, but not so different from here. But we know better, don't we? Understanding a culture other than your own takes some kind of immersion in it, enough time at least that you can look past easy stereotypes.

If you want to find the best place to stay in Dubai, take a peek at Lonely Planet's guide, but if you want to learn about the Land of the Self, read an insightful writer's account of Dubai, such as George Saunders's essay "The New Mecca." The problem with guidebooks is that they suggest objectivity, when in fact the author might have hidden agendas and biases that he's unwilling or afraid to share with the reader, as Thomas Kohnstamm showed in *Do Travel Writers Go to Hell?* in which he exposes travel writing's tawdry side.

In the old days of travel writing, an infiltrator was truly that, a spy in another culture. One of the great adventurers of his time, the Victorian writer, translator, and daredevil Sir Richard Burton, has long been someone I've been fascinated with. Not only did he know twenty-six languages, but he brought the *Tales of the Arabian Nights* to the West with his translation, as well as the famous Indian sexual treatise, *The Kama Sutra*. There are few who have immersed themselves more in other cultures than Burton, and with unparalleled curiosity and respect for other cultures, for a man born into Victorian England. He was one of the first nonbelievers to ever gain access to the holy city of Mecca. While stationed in the British army in India, he had studied the Koran and learned Arabic, and then he took leave from the army and traveled to Egypt, where he posed as a Muslim traveler. From there, he joined a caravan and made his way to Mecca.

The world of course has changed, and today, such an adventure would be widely condemned. But this was before CNN and before the Internet, and British adventurers tended to wander anywhere they chose, as the world was their imperial oyster, but I'd argue that Burton's sacrilegious foray into Mecca was mostly for the good, in that it aimed at understanding and was for the most part respectful. Yes, he *does* refer to the worshippers at Mecca as "fanatics," but in all respects he went much farther than most infidels in trying to understand a group of people so different from the narrow-minded imperial Englishmen with whom he had been schooled.

A crowd had gathered round the Ka'abah, and I had no wish to stand bareheaded and barefooted in the midday September sun. At the cry of "Open a path for the Haji who would enter the House!" the gazers made way. Two stout Meccans, who stood below the door, raised me in their arms, whilst a third drew me from above into the building. At the entrance I was accosted by several officials, dark-looking Meccans, of whom the blackest and plainest was a youth of the Benu Shaybah fam-

ily, the *sangre azul* of Al Hijiz. He held in his hand the huge silver-gilt
padlock of the Ka'abah, and presently, taking his seat upon a kind of
wooden press in the left corner of the hall, he officially inquired my
name, nation, and others particulars. The replies were satisfactory, and
the boy Mohammed was authoritatively ordered to conduct me round
the building, and to recite the prayers. I will not deny that, looking at the
windowless walls, the officials at the door, and a crowd of excited fanatics below ... my feelings were of the trapped-rat description, ... This
did not, however, prevent my carefully observing the scene during our
long prayers, and making a rough plan with a pencil upon my white
Ihram. (206–07)

In "The New Mecca," George Saunders, on assignment for *GQ*, travels
to Dubai to sample some of the most luxurious hotels in the world, including the world's only seven-star hotel, the Burj Al Arab. (The essay
is reprinted in his book *The Braindead Megaphone*.) This is the cushy
assignment we all dream about, akin to the aforementioned Dagmar
flying us in the corporate jet to Kuala Lumpur, from where we'll take
a launch to a seven-star hotel made of endangered coral. Most of us
would kill for such an assignment, but Saunders doesn't make it seem
as pleasurable as all that, and that's why it's so fun to read.

Saunders is in no way a Sir Richard Burton. He claims before the trip
not even to know the location of Dubai, and it's not so much Dubai
we learn about as Saunders *in* Dubai. From the beginning, he seems
unsettled and ill at ease in this land of extreme wealth, striking up conversations with cabbies and guest workers. Saunders wanders around
the luxurious environs of Dubai in a perpetual state of confusion/
exhilaration/despair, a kind of literary culture shock in which he con-
veys to the reader his inability to truly understand Dubai or any other
place on earth as a "concept," even though the city packages itself as a
grouping of concepts that can be purchased if the consumer has enough
money. There's the giant indoor ski slope with manufactured snow, the
nightclubs full of wealthy businessmen and prostitutes, the Al Maha resort located within a desert preserve. Saunders navigates them all with
the same sense of trepidation that Burton felt in the real Mecca. He

even runs into financial troubles—when there's a glitch in his room payment, the front desk at the Burj Al Arab keeps calling to politely but insistently demand when he'll be settling his bill. Saunders feels his status as infidel acutely, the idea that he's somehow an impostor and might be unmasked at any moment:

> I resisted the urge to crawl under the bed. I experienced a sudden fear that a group of Disapproving Guest Services People would appear at my remote-controlled door and physically escort me down to the lobby ATM (an ATM about which I expect I'll be having anxiety nightmares the rest of my life), which would once again prominently display the words *Provider Declines Transaction*. It's true what the Buddhists say: Mind can convert Heaven into Hell. This was happening to me. A headline in one of the nine complimentary newspapers read, actually read: "American jailed for Nonpayment of Hotel Bill."
>
> Perhaps someone had put acid in the complimentary Evian? (40)

As Saunders shows, the travel writer doesn't *have* to be an expert in the destination about which he's writing, though in less capable hands the trope of the bumbling outsider can grow tiresome quickly, especially if the bumbling persona starts to seem lazy or disrespectful. What a difference it would make if Saunders were writing about Chiapas, Mexico, and not Dubai. If he didn't bother to find out anything about the area's poverty and history of rebellion, it would be difficult to write an essay of any merit about the place. It's doubtful *GQ* would have any interest in Chiapas, in any event.

Regardless, the country of yourself has to be conveyed as sharply and honestly as possible for the reader to care about it. The real infiltration here becomes the reader's infiltration into your psyche. The writer Philip Graham claims that every book is in some ways a travel book. It's a useful way in which to think of your writing, whether or not you're writing travel literature. The country of yourself can be explored as fruitfully as any country outside of yourself. There's always some place you're going in your writing, some destination of which you had no idea when you started. Writing is transformative in the same way that travel is.

Still, that's not the same as saying that the place about which you're writing is less important than you. That would indeed be a self-indulgent attitude. It's important to approach your subject with a sense of humility and the certainty that it *is* a real place and not just a figment of your imagination. All that's being pointed out here is that the place is necessarily filtered through your imagination and past experiences and cultural baggage, and so part of your visit includes an understanding of who you are, too.

There's hardly a more self-investigative travel book than Jan Morris's *Trieste and the Meaning of Nowhere*. As the title suggests, the book is about more than the city of Trieste in northern Italy; it's also about the fragility of identity. Directly below the book's dedication are the words, "Jan Morris lived and wrote as James Morris until she completed a change of sexual role in 1972." While the author's sex change is not the overt subject of the book, it's very much a part of the larger territory the book covers. To understand this, we have to understand the nature of the city of Trieste, a city that has changed hands many times over the centuries and was, from 1382 until the end of World War I, part of the Austro-Hungarian Empire. If you go to Trieste, as I have with Morris's book in hand, and stroll around the Piazza dell'Unità d'Italia, the last thing you think about is how Italian everything seems, despite the plaza's name (which seems more of a pouty assertion than a genuine claim). The buildings surrounding the piazza are all Hapsburg-era and have a kind of Austrian tidiness about them. The gentlemen statues around the piazza are all Hapsburg monarchs, and the stylish Italians sipping their Aperol spritzes at sunset while glancing every now and then at the Bay of Trieste, dominated by its various superliners in port, do little to brush aside a kind of odd nostalgia for a vanished and mostly forgotten empire, which seems, in retrospect, less harmful than most others. The local Slovenes (Trieste is virtually surrounded by Slovenia) still refer to the piazza as *Veliki trg* (Great Square), and you're liable to see the occasional slash of graffiti on an overpass claiming Trieste as Slovenian. Until World War I, Trieste was *the* great port of the Austro-Hungarian empire, but it hardly rates as an important port in modern Italy.

Into this city, suffering from an identity crisis, marched young James Morris as an occupying British soldier in 1945. It's not nostalgia for empire that makes Morris's book such a strong evocation of place and history, but her deep understanding, both culturally and personally, of occupying a space that fits comfortably nowhere . . . as the title suggests. Along the way she explores the various travelers who have passed through the city, including the hapless Hapsburg royal Maximilian, drafted by his family to become emperor of Mexico. He much would have preferred staying home and tending to his garden than lording it over Mexico, a sentiment shared by the Mexicans who propped him against a wall and shot him, when a simple "no thank you" might have sufficed. Maximilian left behind a widow who went mad and a beautiful castle and gardens in Trieste, Miramar. James Joyce and Sir Richard Burton lived in this city of exiles as well. One of my favorite passages in *Trieste* concerns Burton's proper and somewhat scandalized widow burning his papers in their courtyard shortly after his death.

> Some days after the Consul's [Burton's] death, nosy passers-by looking through a window might have seen a bright fire burning in a bedroom grate, and Isabel passionately throwing papers into it—as though an enemy were at the gates, and she must destroy the consulate documents. In fact, she was putting to the flames the two manuscript volumes of his unfinished final translation of *The Scented Garden*, said to be one of the most sensuously beautiful of all Arabic poems, with a commentary of his own rich in sexual scholarship. Burton himself said the book would be the crown of his life, but Isabel thought she could hardly do less than burn it, for the sake of Richard's soul and reputation. (136)

It strikes me that Morris has two things going for her, as demonstrated by the passage above, that any travel writer worth the ticket must have if she wants to be more than a tourist, but an insider as well: *authority* and an ability to convey *context*.

Authority can be a murky concept to convey. It's simply the sense that the writer knows what he's talking about and is convincing.

If the place is the place of your birth, where you grew up, and where your ancestors lived and died, than the context is simple to provide. But if the place is somewhere you stumbled upon, then you might not be so sure why it's so important to you. Sometimes it takes a lifetime to figure out, as was the case with Jan Morris.

What the importance of a place is to you can be one of the most profound questions of your life. Fifteen years ago, I never would have imagined that the Philippines would play an important role in my life. When I was fourteen and saw a documentary on the Tasaday people who lived supposedly idyllic lives in the Philippines rainforest, I remember imagining what it might be like to go there, never dreaming I would do just that twenty-five years later. When I was sixteen, my older brother and I applied to be summer volunteers working for the shady (I later learned) Philippine government organization PANAMIN, who were the gatekeepers to the Tasaday rainforest. Nothing came of it because the head of PANAMIN, the mercurial and autocratic Manuel Elizalde, Jr., closed it down. But at that time the Philippines meant next to nothing to me. I was a little disappointed that I didn't get to traipse around the jungle for the summer (though I'm pretty sure my mother wouldn't have allowed me to go in the end), but a year later, I became an exchange student in Japan, and the Philippine jungle was forgotten until 1997, when I started my research on my book *Invented Eden*. Along the way, I read whatever I could get my hands on about the Philippines, because I had a steep learning curve. Inevitably, I knew that whatever I said about the Tasaday could not be taken out of the cultural context of the Philippines, and I knew next to nothing about that vast and complex country, a fact that fairly stuns me now with my own audacity and naïveté, to say nothing of the reckless faith in me displayed by my publisher.

Filipinos and non Filipinos alike recommended to me one writer in particular to get up to speed: the British writer James Hamilton-Paterson, who had lived for a number of years in a remote village in the Visayan region of the country, and had all the authority I lacked. A couple of years into my investigation, after I'd talked to a score of anthropologists and journalists involved on one side of the Tasaday story or the other, and after I'd spent months cumulatively in the Philippines and had met the Tasaday twice, I took my friends' advice and read

Hamilton-Paterson's investigation of the Marcos dictatorship: *America's Boy*. The book alternated between a sweeping history of the Marcos years, including a wonderful scene in which Hamilton-Paterson dines with the late dictator's widow, the notorious Imelda Marcos, and village life in a place Hamilton-Paterson calls Kansulay. In this way, he was able to ingeniously comment on the trickle-down effect (almost nil) of the Marcos government on the way of life of villagers who were more affected by their overseas relatives sending home appliances than the various edicts of Ferdinand Marcos. I admired the book, except for one chapter that touched on the Tasaday. I thought he had got it all wrong, dismissing the Tasaday as a bald hoax, end of story.

A bit nervy of me, but I tracked down Mr. Hamilton-Paterson's e-mail address with the help of a mutual friend, and wrote to tell him that for all his brilliance he had missed the mark completely on the issue of the Tasaday. When I didn't hear back from him for several months, I sent a follow-up, gently chiding him for not responding but wishing him well. To my astonishment, he replied to this e-mail, apologizing because he had been traveling, and to my further astonishment, he admitted that the chapter on the Tasaday was the only one in the book he regretted. He had been rushed and had simply taken the word of some of his friends on the story. I mention this to illustrate that in a sense all of literature is a conversation between writers and scholars through the ages. The responses typically come slowly, across generations, but occasionally, the conversation happens in real time, as happened between James Hamilton-Paterson and myself.

When my book was finished, my publisher sent Hamilton-Paterson a copy, and this author I admired did something almost unheard of. He admitted he'd been wrong. In print. Writing in the *London Review of Books*, Hamilton-Paterson apologized—not to me, but to John Nance, the former Associated Press photographer who wrote the bestselling book *The Gentle Tasaday* in 1975, and who was roundly condemned as a dupe and a liar when the hoax allegations surfaced in 1986. The review, I should add, was largely positive, but Hamilton-Paterson had his quibbles with my book, just as I had had with his. So goes it. All a part of the ongoing conversation.

All this leads to another question. How did an upper-class Brit, son of a doctor and an anesthesiologist, wind up living in a remote Philippine village for a good portion of his life? My teacher, the late short-story writer and novelist Barry Hannah, once told me that what I needed to know about writing was this: "Write honestly about what you love and put a little music in it." This is good advice. But what you love isn't always what you know. Sometimes what you love is what you discover, something that completes you in the same way that each partner in a good marriage is said to complete the other. In the case of James Hamilton-Paterson, he describes in a book almost entirely about Kansulay, *Playing with Water*, a quasi-mystical episode in which he discovers a drawing he made in a French notebook from 1953 that seemed to prefigure by thirty years his arrival on the island:

> For there on the ruled paper was a drawing of Tiwarik, an island in the Philippines I had first set eyes on only two years before. True, the map was not correct in every detail, but in its main features—outline, peak, a grassfield—it was probably as good a map as I could have produced at that age had I been drawing it from actual memory.
>
> This discovery made a silent concussion in my life. For a week I was bemused . . . What had happened? Had I had some psychic prefiguring of a place I was destined to visit? Or once having invented somewhere had I doomed thirty years of my life to discovering its analogue?
>
> There is a third possibility which I now think is the most likely explanation. The shape I drew was not dreamed up that far-off June day but had existed for me since infancy in a rudimentary way . . . I was not in search of a physical counterpart . . . not even unconsciously. But when I stumbled on one called Tiwarik there was an instant and profound recognition. Later the chance finding of my boyhood doodle showed me a shape I had once seen so clearly and had forgotten. (4)

This passage reminds me of a quote from Walter Benjamin, who wrote, "The fairy in whose presence we are granted a wish is there for each of us. But few of us know how to remember the wish we have made; and so, few of us recognize its fulfillment later in our lives" (61).

Sometimes a place we discover in the world works like that, as a wish we didn't even know we had wished, fulfilled. It's from this fulfillment or perhaps the search for this fulfillment that writers as insightful as Jan Morris and James Hamilton-Paterson write. Neither were born as insiders in the places which they write about, but they spent years picking up the nuances of place that people born and bred there might overlook or take for granted.

I'm not saying that you must live in a place for years, or visit it many times, before you have the right or ability to say anything new about it. Saunders writes insightfully of Dubai after only a short visit, and Joan Didion famously wrote an important book on El Salvador after spending only two weeks there.

Almost by definition, travel books and essays are written by outsiders, and the audience is an outsider audience, but with the advent of the Internet, that's all changed, and an outsider's travel piece might be read by insiders as much as by outsiders. But one kind of travel book that can't be replicated by an outsider, no matter how much inside information she possesses, is the book or essay written by an exile or expatriate. The insider looking back on her own culture shouldn't escape our attention. I'm not referring to the "heritage traveler," someone returning to a country that was home to her ancestors. I'm referring to the writer who moved away from the land of his birth when he was a young man and has now returned to that country to take a second look, to see what has changed and what hasn't, to tell us about the little store that used to sit at that corner, and the clear spring that now is a polluted creek in a filthy shanty town.

The insider who returns to his country not only has inside knowledge that the outsider can never have, but also has the outsider's knowledge (which is more graspable) and can often see the old country with a clearer eye than the person who has never left the homeland. Writers who haven't left their home country are almost always highly critical of those who do. Some Indian writers I've met disdain Jhumpa Lahiri, the Pulitzer-Prize-winning author born in London, but raised in the U.S. While some of this can be safely categorized as envy, it can't be completely dismissed. They disdain her because she's not telling them anything new (and yes, I know she's writing fiction and our discussion so far has involved nonfiction, but this is still relevant). Of course she's not telling them anything new . . . culturally. She's not writing for an Indian audience. She's writing for a non-Indian American and European audience. She straddles more than one culture, and so what she gives us we might call a cultural translation. She's translating Indian culture to a Western audience. I've heard Chinese and Filipino writers express the same disdain for writers who are writing *about* Chinese or Filipino culture but not *for* these cultures.

The case of Luis Francia might be an exception. Here's a Filipino expatriate, a long-time resident of New York City, who is widely respected in the Philippines and the U.S. His book *Eye of The Fish* is an extended meditation/travelogue on the land of his birth, in which he takes us from one end of the Philippine Archipelago to the other, sorting through memories of his childhood along the way, as well as life in New York.

On a Jeepney on one of the trips that thread through the book, Francia travels to one of the poorest Philippine islands, Leyte, home of a famous World War II naval battle and birthplace of Imelda Marcos, one of the richest people in the world. He's on his way to visit Eliza, the niece of a friend from New York. Note how he writes as both insider and outsider simultaneously. I'd say he's writing for an American audience (which of course includes Filipino Americans), as well as a Filipino audience as he reflects on life in New York. In this long passage, notice how he moves from insider to outsider briefly, and back again to insider:

We drive along the eastern edge of Leyte, the Pacific Ocean to our right. Palmyras interpose themselves between traveler and the sea, a tide that waits for no one. The towns on the coast are spread out, with nothing but coconut groves and trees and the shore between. There are interludes of verdant rice and cornfields, the bright green fed by the rains that will continue to bless the parched earth until late October. Sometimes, rounding a curve on a hill, we see the coast undulate before us, merging with the iridescent waters. Occasionally an island appears in the near distance, almost like a mirage, like the generic tropical isles travel posters have made synonymous with stress-free vacations: green rows of palmyras and coconut trees, desolate white beaches, calm blue-green waters. The promise of obedient natives, their bare brown skin shimmering with health and their smiling guileless faces eloquently hinting at sex without tears—joyous jumping-up-and-down sex, sex for the heaven of it—lies just below the surface, the titillations of a land-scape sans guilt, a landscape expunged of inconvenient details, a tabula rasa upon which Western fantasies about the dangerous but delicious eroticism of darkness are projected.

The men and women who live here are indeed dark, but wish for the most part that they weren't, not so much because they fear the sun but simply because dark serves light, an inherent injustice they have known all their lives. In their mutual dissatisfaction, light and dark find some kind of dialogue, not in any yin-yang way, but in the only realm left in the late twentieth century where such dialogue is guaranteed: commerce. Such interaction is flawed, however, because it is weighed heavily in favor of light, source of largesse, whose motto is, Give the money and run. To the dark-skinned men and women, the taking of the money engenders a certain resentment, for the business of exoticization ties them down to these parts. To them, the sight of these islands does not evoke pastoral dreams but rather the opposite, the hardship of a life with precious little water even though they are surrounded by it, of working land that is barely arable, a hunk of rock and sand thrown up by the sea, a waystation for someplace else—if there were someplace else. The people who live here, as Derek Walcott writes of his own beloved Caribbean folk, "are not there to be loved or even photographed; they are trees who sweat."

In the dreary winters of New York, I often envision such islands, se-duced—perhaps I should say brainwashed—by the delirious promise of abandonment both psychic and physical, of being cut off from the moorings of a claustrophobic and artificial environment, not so much to rule over a patch of earth as to be a part of it. In the islander that I am (and is it just coincidence that my second home is an island as well?) there are strong hints of the pagan, the animist, as there are in other islanders here. Living at the edge of the sea breeds an intuitive sense that somewhere deep within us are the remnants of fish-consciousness, a piscine, subaqueous feeling for the abyss. Well aware of being separate from continents, we glorify this condition, looking upon the vast intervals of water as moats protecting delicate kingdoms. (156–57)

All journeys begin first in the imagination. For the exile returning home, the imagined journey combines with remembered journeys and finally mixes into a combustible potion when added to the present-day experience when his plane lands or his boat docks on ground that is both *terra firma* and *terra incognita* at once.

Such a journey is inevitably imbued with wistfulness. It's hard to imagine it otherwise. The way things have gone on earth the last hundred years, most landscapes have deteriorated, not improved. But the *Balikbayan* (in Tagalog, a word meaning a person returning to his homeland) has to get beyond mere wistfulness. Longing for the good old days is generally something that can't be communicated well to someone who wasn't there, and of course, the good old days were most often not as good as remembered.

The writer Stephanie Elizondo Griest advocates solo travel as the most rewarding, and I tend to agree. While I love traveling with my family, it's when I'm alone that I'm best able to understand who I am in the world. To not belong somewhere forces the lone traveler to better understand where, if anywhere, he feels settled. As G. K. Chesterton wrote in his essay "The Riddle of the Ivy": "The whole object of travel is not to set foot on foreign land; it is at last to set foot on one's own country as a foreign land" (http://www.readbookonline.net/readOnLine/20697/). You could also substitute the word *self* for *country* in that sentence and it would have as much meaning: "The whole object of travel is not to set foot on foreign land; it is at last to set foot in oneself as a foreign land."

The Quest

A quest often implies some kind of spiritual journey, but not always. A quest can involve a search for identity or origin, or it might involve a principle or ideal, though not necessarily spiritual in nature. Can an atheist or agnostic go on a quest? You bet. Consider Sarah Vowell's immensely readable quest (she calls it a pilgrimage; the two aren't quite the same, but close enough), *Assassination Vacation*, in which she visits virtually every shrine and obscure way station involved with various presidential assassinations, from the Ford Theater, where John Wilkes Booth shot Abraham Lincoln, to the Dry Tortugas, where Dr. Samuel Mudd, the white supremacist physician who treated the wounded Booth, was imprisoned.

Vowell started her project in the midst of the Iraq War and George W. Bush's presidency, and she admits early in the book that she can't even utter his name. She simply refers to him as "the current president" because the word "current" suggests that he won't always be the president. I can't think of any other writer besides Vowell who could make the topic of presidential assassination somehow charming, but she does just that. Not that she's pro-assassination. Not at all, as she stresses in this passage:

> I embarked on the project of touring historic sites and monuments having to do with the assassinations of Lincoln, Garfield, and McKinley right around the time my country iffily went to war, which is to say right around the time my resentment of the current president cranked up into contempt. Not that I want the current president killed . . . I will, for the record (and for the FBI agent assigned to read this and make sure I mean no harm—hello there), clearly state that while I am obsessed with death, I am against it. (6)

What then did she want to do? She wanted to explore the misguided motivations of assassins, from the famous actor John Wilkes Booth, who timed his fatal shot to coincide with a laugh line, to the absolutely insane and cheerful assassin of affable and bookish James Garfield, Charles Guiteau, who expected to be appointed ambassador to France (though he had absolutely no qualifications for the post), to the dour anarchist assassin of McKinley. Curiously, the only assassins that interest her are those who assassinated Republican presidents. While the assassin of Kennedy is mentioned several times in the book, Lee Harvey Oswald seems not to interest her too much. Nope, she's only interested in the assassins of Republicans. The book is almost an anti-quest in this respect, an ironic, humorous, and subtle journey to discover the reasons why she or someone else shouldn't dream of and hope for an assassin to come along and remove from office someone she considers vile. Vowell herself has within her family lineage both people who were the victims of murderers (Native Americans who were marched across the continent along the infamous Trail of Tears) as well as at least one murderer (a relative who participated in the sacking of Lawrence, Kansas, an anti-slavery stronghold, in the days leading up to the Civil War). The book ends with Vowell attending an Easter sunrise service at the Lincoln Memorial, worrying about becoming an unwitting target of terrorists.

I'm going to go against my knee-jerk sense of propriety and say that not all quests need to be deeply felt. Some quests are more earnest than others, and some just seem immediately appealing and fun, such as Michael Paterniti's *Driving Mr. Albert*. The impetus for the story was an urban legend Paterniti had heard, that Albert Einstein's brain was in the possession of a private individual. Indeed, he found this to be true. The pathologist who had removed Einstein's brain during an autopsy in 1955 to "study it," as he claimed, had never returned it. Finally, in his eighties, he was ready to relinquish it when Paterniti found him, and so an unlikely road trip began, a quest not to find Einstein's brain, but to return it.

Who wouldn't see the potential in such a high-concept quest? It's no surprise that this idea first found form as a magazine piece in *Harper's*. It's an immediately likably absurd situation, both bizarre and, in the hands of a capable writer such as Paterniti, likely to yield results that say something meaningful about the culture, rather than only the individual. In a way, a situation such as this, like Vowell's, is a cultural quest rather than a personal one. It's the task of such a writer not only to tell a quirky story, but to look for the relevance of the story in relation to who we are as a society, what we value and what we don't. I'm not saying it's an excuse to sermonize, but that such a story will by its nature need to become allegorical or metaphorical in some sense in order for it to make its mark on the reading public.

It's worth mentioning here that the quest form doesn't have to be written—a quest suggests movement and movement suggests film/video. The low cost of video equipment makes the possibility of filming your quest a lot easier than it used to be. Documentary filmmaker Ross McElwee famously filmed his documentary *Sherman's March* in the 1980s with a hand-held camera, a kind of ironic cinema verité that made for some awkward and hilarious social situations. When his former teacher and sidekick/fairy godmother Charlene tries to set him up on a blind date, he films everything about the encounter as he's introduced to a young woman who obviously thinks she's been set up with a weirdo. "Put the camera down, Ross!" Charlene says, exasperated, but he doesn't, he can't.

If you don't know a documentary filmmaker to record your quest, and you're not one yourself, no matter. The DIY nature of the modern-day quest lends itself to a kind of charming amateurishness to the endeavor. You don't want your film to seem too polished, I think (even if it is) because the quest then seems somehow less authentic. Take as an example the French documentary filmmaker Antoine de Maximy, who has rigged up three cameras attached to his body, two pointed towards him and one pointed away. Talk about a conversation starter! Imagine what it must be to see a gangly man approach you with a smile and three cameras attached to him. In *J'irai Dormir à Hollywood* (which seems awkwardly translated in its English release as *Hollywood, I'm Sleeping Over Tonight*), his quest is one that only a guileless visitor from another country might endeavor to undertake, and for this reason the film has a great deal of charm. First, he decides to travel America only by hitching, Greyhound bus, and (finally and improbably) by hearse, winding up in Hollywood, where it's his goal to sleep in the home of a Hollywood star. Does he know any Hollywood stars? Nope, but no matter. Antoine de Maximy possesses an inordinate amount of chutzpah. Speaking English with a heavy French accent, he approaches complete strangers from New York to Los Angeles and asks if he can stay overnight at their house. What Hollywood star could resist such an approach?

Such a ploy would never occur to a native-born American. It would seem absurd, dangerous, and foolhardy, but that's the point. This is the nature of travel. A foreigner can often get away with something a native never could because of his outsider status, because he's relying on idealized notions of place, and doesn't know better. If God loves fools, he certainly loves Antoine de Maximy, because de Maximy ventures places that might seem off-limits to most Americans. Along the way, de Maximy dances with a group of Hassidic Jews in Manhattan, asks a group of Amish if he can stay overnight with them (they politely decline), saunters through the devastated post-Katrina neighborhoods of New Orleans, and wanders onto a Navajo reservation. At first, he's invited to dinner there and treated courteously if a little warily, but then he's kicked off when the residents decide that his hearse is a bad omen. Eventually, he makes it to Hollywood, where he attempts to gate-crash the homes of various Hollywood stars, winding up instead spending the night alongside a homeless man on the beach.

We could have told Antoine that he wasn't going to get into a star's home, right? And I'm sure that he never actually expected to realize his dream (though he makes it pretty far up a driveway or two). That bit of new-age bumper-sticker speak comes to mind: the journey is the destination. Yep (gag), it's true. Certainly, it's true for the writer or documentarian. Even if de Maximy knew or suspected that he wasn't going to get into a star's home, the goal of the quest was still a valid organizing principle for the adventure. Remember what I said about a cultural quest becoming by its nature allegorical and metaphorical? That's exactly the case with de Maximy's project. It can't help but become a piece about peeling away the façade of the American Dream to reveal the huge gaps between endemic poverty and gated privilege.

When I showed this documentary to a mixed group of American and French college students in France, the American students reacted, unsurprisingly, a little defensively. Frankly, I felt a bit defensive, too, though I recognized this reaction as a knee-jerk response, and one that said more about my blind spots than about the embedded criticism of American society in de Maximy's playful but ultimately scathing film. My American students, mostly from the Midwest, wished that de Maximy had taken a northern route rather than a southern. Yes, that would indeed have been film-worthy. We could have been mesmerized as he ice-fished on Lake Winnebago in Wisconsin. Imagine the antics if he'd run across an insurance adjuster in Des Moines and asked if he could visit his home! The point wasn't to make Americans feel good about themselves. The film's intended audience wasn't even American. A French friend of mine responded, when I told her of the reaction of my class, that de Maximy's route was exactly what most French people would want to see of America, starting in New York, and then communing with various idealized and stereotyped groups: Native Americans, Amish, African Americans, and then winding up in Hollywood.

There's always going to be a certain amount of happenstance in any quest you're involved in. No doubt your fellow travelers will make up a good part of the story, and you never know for sure whom you're going to meet or what adventures or calamities you might endure. Still, a quest is usually something that's willed in advance—you *set off* on a quest. You have an intended goal. But that's not invariably the case. Sometimes a quest sneaks up on you and you don't know you're on one until you're in the midst of it.

The two types of quest most often undertaken are the spiritual and the identity based, and these two realms are the most emotionally fraught and difficult to navigate, much more so than seeking a Hollywood star who will let you crash at his mansion or transporting Einstein's brain from one coast to the other. The word *quest* was coined at the turn of the fourteenth century, at a time when most people rarely left home, and if they did, they had better have had a good idea what they were searching for. A spiritual quest involved, say, finding the Holy Grail or searching for the True Cross, a reinforcement of faith, but never to *find* faith, and certainly never to discover one's roots. If you didn't know where your roots were, you had better not tell anyone. This was the nature of existential crisis, fourteenth-century style: "Don't know who you are, eh? Maybe if we gouge your eyes out, that will jog your memory!" A Spanish Catholic knew he was a Spanish

Catholic and didn't venture east to live in a Tibetan monastery or west to Mexico to figure out, like, the meaning of life, and who he really was. He knew who he was, for better or worse, and didn't even know Mexico existed. If he went to Mexico, as he later did, he did so to conquer on a quest for treasure, and nothing to do with personal identity. Ah, the good old days, right? Maybe, if you're nostalgic for the brutality and narrow-mindedness that goes hand in hand with spiritual and ethnic absolutism. I, for one, am much more comfortable with people who don't know who they are than I am with people who have no doubts. Those people scare me. So it follows that I'm drawn to quests that have uncertainty at their heart. Two such books are Dinty W. Moore's *The Accidental Buddhist* and Stephanie Elizondo Griest's *Mexican Enough*.

In *The Accidental Buddhist*, Moore starts investigating Buddhism in America out of journalistic curiosity. What is the lure of Buddhism for so many Americans, and how has Buddhism been shaped and modi-fied to fit America? Moore tells us early on of his childhood filled with Catholic terrors, nuns who beat him and filled his young mind with visions of hell. By the time he starts his investigation, he no longer con-siders himself a Catholic; what he considers himself is up for grabs, confused and unhappy and beaten down by dissatisfactions and what the Buddhists term the everyday chatterings of the "monkey mind." So when he goes on his first Buddhist retreat, his curiosity soon turns into obsession. Before long he's embarked on what he calls his American Buddhism Project with all the zeal of a typical type-A American. He subscribes to every Buddhist newspaper and magazine he can lay his hands on. He dutifully goes on retreats and wants to be the best medita-tor he can be! Very American. Not so Buddhist. But it makes for a fun road trip as he ricochets across the country with a kind of self-mocking tone that *does* seem rather Buddhist in that Buddhists are not supposed to take themselves too seriously. And happily, Moore doesn't. Even when he feels he's failed on his quest, his resignation itself is charming and somehow indicative that he hasn't after all failed.

> My various Buddhist experiences have certainly changed me in one way—I get up before dawn most days, whether I need to or not.

As if to stress the paucity of my experience on this failed expedition, a bearded, portly fellow named Keith is the only one who shows up at the center that morning to join me. We sit, just the two of us, in a small room — it probably used to be a bedroom, back when this used to be a house — under an antique light fixture.

Keith isn't even sure how to work the timer, and doesn't know the ceremonial Zen chants that usually open the meditation session. He is worried about this, but I convince him I don't really care.

I don't. We just sit, and listen to the birds wake up.

And you know what? It's the nicest hour of my trip. (170)

In fact, Moore seems to be the perfect messenger for Buddhism in America — irreverent, uncertain, mischievous, and doubting, not so unlike the main character in *Monkey*, the famous Buddhist quest novel by Wu Cheng'en, also known as *Journey to the West*, that I read in college, about an irreverent, uncertain, mischievous, and doubting monkey who travels to India from China to retrieve some holy texts. The best quests, in my experience, always involve a sense of humor and a protagonist who can laugh at his own foibles. Moore might not meet any bodhisattvas along the way or gain enlightenment and immortality (I don't think!), but that, after all, is expecting an awful lot.

Stephanie Elizondo Griest also doesn't discover she's on a quest until she's well into it. Growing up in Corpus Christi, Texas, with an Anglo father and a Mexican American mother, she identifies mostly with her Anglo side through most of her childhood. In grade school, she associates the Mexican kids who don't know English well with slow learners, and she's anything but a slow learner. When it suits her to identify with her Mexican American side, for scholarships, she unhesitatingly does so, and soon receives an offer for a free ride at the University of Texas at Austin. Overwhelmed by guilt at switching from a white identity to a Hispanic one when it suits her, she decides to Mexify herself, decorating her dorm room with posters of Frida Kahlo and the Virgen de Guadalupe. "I taught English to Mexican kids," she writes, "and drank lots of margaritas. I changed my white-bread middle name (Ann) to my mother's maiden name (Elizondo) and made everyone use it. I even got a Colombian boyfriend (bad idea)" (6–7).

A decade goes by. And of course a lot happens in this decade, including her first book, *Around the Bloc: My Life in Moscow, Beijing, and Havana*. An intrepid traveler from the start, she learns Russian and visits Cuba, but her lack of Spanish troubles her. Living now in New York City, she cycles through Spanish lessons to no avail. Then on her thirtieth birthday, she steps off the subway at the wrong station and sees a travel poster with the words, *I want to go to Mexico*. Before she has a chance to have a change of heart, she books a ticket.

Now that's my kind of quest, a kind of *I Ching*, throw-your-destiny-up-in-the-air-and-see-where-it-lands quest. Of course, such quests don't always work out well, and when they don't you're more likely to become the subject of someone else's narrative rather than the author of your own. Think: *Into the Wild*, Christopher McCandless, and Jon Krakauer. So it's good to have some notion of where you're headed, a credit card that isn't maxed out, generous friends and relatives, map-reading skills, and barring all that, the blind (or at least clouded) faith of an Antoine de Maximy or a Stephanie Elizondo Griest.

The Reenactment

Travel is ripe for the reenactment. Nearly every year, someone gets the idea to reenact someone else's famous voyage, film it, and write about it. Sometimes, the idea is to prove or disprove a theory, such as Thor Heyerdahl's famous voyage of the Kon Tiki in 1947, in which the explorer set off on a raft across the Pacific from Peru in order to prove his theory that it was possible for pre-Columbian peoples from South America to have settled Polynesia. And the intrepid Nellie Bly caused a world sensation by reenacting in the late nineteenth century Jules Verne's fictional travel chronicle, *Around the World in 80 Days*.

A reenactment suggests an original voyage that was either famous, overlooked, or unrecorded (as in the original voyagers of Thor Heyerdahl's theory). But you don't have to find a famous voyage to reenact.

Most of the famous voyages (Columbus, the Pilgrims), but not all, have been reenacted at one time or another, and in any case, there aren't many people with the resources to build ancient ships to scale and attempt such a reenactment. If you *are* one of those people whose wish is everyone else's command, congratulations (and if you need another crew member, please get in touch with me). There's no reason why you can't reenact something considerably less famous, perhaps something not famous at all, but much more meaningful. Tom Bissell, for instance, reenacted in a sense his father's service during the Vietnam War in *The Father of All Things: A Marine, His Son, and the Legacy of Vietnam.* At the heart of this book is a trip Bissell took with his father, a lieutenant during the war, back to Vietnam. The book is not only a travel memoir but a well-researched history of the war in which Bissell reevaluates the gross mistakes, multiple tragedies, and miscalculations made by the upper echelons of the U.S. military and political establishment.

One thing I've tried to make clear in this book is that most often an immersion project's worth can be measured by how high the stakes are. Obviously, the stakes are high for Bissell—this isn't just another Vietnam history or memoir, but a look at the war through the eyes of a son who doesn't always get along with his father. In fact, relations between the two are strained throughout the book, and Bissell sometimes regresses, as we all do when we're around our parents, to the essentials of any meaningful parent/child relationship: whininess and sulkiness. Personally, I love that. I tell my students not to make themselves the heroes of their own memoirs. If you do, people won't trust you as a narrator.

The stakes are always high when we're writing about our parents. They inhabited a world before we were born and their story is our Origin Story. We are always measuring ourselves up to the mythic, sometimes hazy lives of our parents. And Bissell is no exception—in understanding the war, he starts to understand his father. In taking a trip to Vietnam with his father, he starts to understand the war. At one point, he and his father visit the Cu Chi Tunnels, a labyrinth where Viet Cong lived and died by the thousands, heavily bombarded by the U.S. and searched out by so-called tunnel rats (U.S. troops as well as Australian and New Zealand troops who squirmed through the narrow and dark tunnels to kill Viet Cong). When I visited the tunnels several years ago, my stakes were largely cultural. I was seventeen when the North Vietnamese drove their tanks into the presidential palace grounds in Saigon and the country was reunited, the war lost, from the American perspective. I had grown up in opposition to the war, but no one in my family had served in it. My father had served in World War II and my older brother's draft number was high enough that he escaped the draft. But it's hard enough being an American visitor to Ho Chi Minh City without a veteran in tow. My wife and I visited Cu Chi on a tour led by an ex-Viet-Cong guy born in 1947 named Tung, whose mother, sister, and brother had been killed by Americans not so very different from me. Tung took a special interest in me. Every fifteen minutes or so he'd belt out an impromptu song about what we were going to see. The songs were always sung to the tune of "Auld Lang Syne." He also made me (and only me) feel the impossibly deep war wound on his shoulder— he had been shot by an American gunship during the Tet Offensive and had nearly died. And I had to listen to one antic, guilt-inspiring lyric after another, sung at full tilt with a full-on smile. "And now we're going to see the village where the Americans committed unspeakable atrocities!" Try singing *that* to "Auld Lang Syne."

I didn't even want to go in the Cu Chi tunnels when Tung invited me to do so. I didn't think I could fit, and I don't as a rule like to go into dark, tight places with former enemies. But I went. When I emerged from the double-wide Fat American tunnel (not its official name), I heard in the near distance the unmistakable sound of gunfire. As Tung led us to the inevitable American Atrocity Gift Shop, the sounds of gunfire grew closer until it became clear that there was a firing range, and one of the main gifts you could take home from the gift shop was the precious memory of firing off an AK-47, that and hearing loss. Truly, I had never before heard a sound so deafening. As Margie and I passed the firing range, I felt real terror of the kind I had not experienced many times. These were not the polite muffled bullet sounds of the movies. I learned that afternoon that the sound of scores of bullets and small explosives fired at close range is in itself a wound. It might not pierce your skin, but it's something that I can't imagine easily recovering from, even if one never strikes you in the chaos of battle. I couldn't comprehend what it must have been like to even move in the face of such an aural onslaught. When Tung asked me in his cheerful manner whether I'd like to shoot a gun, I shook my head. I just wanted to get out of there.

Not so Tom Bissell. In that same spot, with his father along, Bissell decided he wanted to shoot an AK-47. Perhaps in Bissell's shoes, I would have wanted to do the same. In that desire to shoot a gun on his father's battlefield, as it were, Bissell is engaging himself and the reader in a complex psychodrama. In some ways, we all refight our parents' battles, and re-engage our parents in battle, dead or alive, for our entire lives. Tom Bissell does so in a more literal sense than most of us. I had no reason to fire a gun at the shooting range beside the Cu Chi tunnels, no emotional investment, but Bissell does. And Bissell's father reminds his son at that moment that he has an even greater emotional investment in such a reenactment. Bissell writes, "'Now imagine,' my father piped up, 'that 20 guys are firing back at you, and people everywhere are screaming'" (344).

Another case in point is Tony Maniaty's reenactment of an infamous event in Australian history, one that he was intimately involved with. In 1975, Maniaty was a young television journalist working for the Australian Broadcasting Corporation (ABC) who was sent over to the Portuguese colony of East Timor, just a few hundred kilometers off the coast of northern Australia, to cover a brewing crisis. Portugal, at the time, was getting out of the colonizing business, divesting itself unceremoniously of its colonies in Africa and in Timor, pulling out without any thought for the people it had ruled for four hundred years (in the case of tiny East Timor). In the vacuum Portugal's departure created, a faction of left-leaning freedom fighters known as Fretilin stepped in, though they were wholly unprepared to govern at the time. Indonesia, which ruled the other half of Timor, coveted the eastern part, and began a troop buildup on the border. Australia, undergoing a constitutional crisis at the time, barely took note. America, fresh from its defeat in Vietnam, and allied with Indonesian strongman Suharto, had no appetite for intervention. The same was true of the Brits. Maniaty was the first to bring in a film crew, and he joined the Fretilin forces in a dusty border town called Balibo to see what would happen, and, in the meantime, filed a number of even-handed reports that the Indonesians did not seem to think were even-handed at all. The Indonesians did not want to be seen as involved; they tried to make it look as though the only fighters involved were Fretilin's rival, the UDT, which favored unification with Indonesia. One morning, the Indonesians lobbed some artillery shells over Maniaty's head as he was doing a report from the top of the old fort that overlooked the Indonesian positions, and then sent a helicopter gunship to try to finish off the job. Maniaty narrowly escaped and then hightailed it back to the relative safety of the East Timor capitol of Dili. On his way back to Dili, he met a news crew from a rival Australian station, heading for Balibo. Invasion seemed imminent, and he told them that if they valued their lives, they should wait until the situation cooled. But for various reasons, they decided not to heed his warnings. Yet another crew joined the first in Balibo, once again against Maniaty's warnings. Within a few days, the five Australian newsmen were dead, executed while trying to surrender to Indonesian troops who overran the tiny outpost.

Maniaty hung around in Dili as long as possible before leaving for Australia in advance of the full-scale invasion. After his return to Australia, he was approached by a fifty-two-year-old journalist named Roger East who had got wind of the story of the missing journalists and wanted to find out their fate. Maniaty warned East not to travel to East Timor in search of the journalists, but once again, his warning went unheeded. Maniaty seemed to understand what the others could not, that the Indonesians did not take kindly to foreign journalists who reported things that did not support Indonesia's version of events. When the Indonesians launched their full-scale invasion of East Timor in December 1975, they dragged East down to the Dili wharf and shot him.

The Indonesian occupation, which lasted until 1999, was brutal. By some estimates, the Indonesians killed a third or more of the East Timorese population, hundreds of thousands of people, engaged in mass rapes, and left as brutally as they had entered after the battered people of the former Portuguese territory pluckily voted for independence. A few dead foreign journalists meant nothing to the Indonesian military. But it meant a great deal to the Australian public, and it's an event that has haunted the country all this time.

In *Shooting Balibo*, Maniaty tells the story of his return after a thirty-some-year absence to this tiny and troubled country. He's there because his friend the director Robert Connolly is shooting a film about the Balibo Five and Roger East and he's brought Maniaty along as a consultant. As travel reenactments go, this is a gem. The book alternates between Maniaty's chronicle of the filming and his memories of the events as he experienced them in 1975. He stays in the same fifty-room hotel in which he lodged in 1975, the Turismo, and is inadvertently given the same room he stayed in back then. He even finds out that the actor playing him in the movie visited East Timor a couple of years earlier and was also given room eleven. Spooky. But that's the kind of thing that happens with reenactments.

It's not only Maniaty who is reliving the past through this movie shot on location, but the East Timorese people, many of whom have been hired as extras. They, too, have an emotional stake in the reenactment, as you can see in the following passage in which he describes a scene being filmed.

Next, only the women will perform, although a male body is required. 'This is where the village women come out and place flowers on the grave.' The men jump forward as volunteers; the women must flail themselves on the body. Everyone is laughing at the sexual context, some mocking the act itself, and Rob struggles to regain control. 'Come on, no laughing,' he says, laughing too. 'This is deadly serious. Okay, ready, and action . . .'

The laughter stops. The women start sobbing, at first quietly, randomly, and then louder, each sob crossing into another, into a wall of sobbing. And then the wailing begins, isolated cries, and then more, undercut with sobbing, until the room is filled with a funereal wailing and weeping, and Rob is nodding encouragement. It's what he wants, strong and beautiful. He's willing them for more and louder, and they turn their rehearsal space, vast and echoing, into a cathedral of suffering and tears. From the side, I realize that even I'm seeing the dead guy as really dead, and the women as real mourners, and the space as a real cemetery. 'And cut,' Rob calls emphatically. But nothing changes. The wailing continues, the women don't stop crying, and the eldest of them, a fine-boned woman called Domingas, is comforted by the others, her tears real and flowing, until gradually she's brought, still sobbing, back to earth.

'Let's take a break,' says Rob quietly. Years of brutality, torture and death have been released, and captured on Ann's recorder. The three of us are reduced to an awkward humility. The actors, pulling back to reality, remain silent. I suddenly feel uncomfortable, an intruder on their sadness. Attempting to make conversation, I ask one of the Timorese what his T-shirt says. He looks down at it. 'Harden the fuck up,' he says, 'in Tetum.' Everyone bursts into laughter. (24–25).

Throughout the book, Maniaty overlays his memories of East Timor, circa 1975, on top of Timor, 2008. As in any good travel book, the experience of reading Maniaty's accounts not only transports the reader to a place most of us will never experience, but into Maniaty's consciousness and personal history. Maniaty scrupulously avoids easy judgments and generalizations; it's his journalistic training, no doubt, that brings a kind of quiet and restrained dignity to his descriptions of the people and places of East Timor. The book is never about him alone; he tries desperately hard and with great compassion to understand the men whose deaths he tried to prevent with his warnings.

Of course, you don't have to visit a site of trauma for a travel reenactment, but it's an option, as Maniaty's and Bissell's examples show, just as it's an option to recreate a famous journey. But you might also consider recreating your own journey. Not that you have to be Paul Theroux to do it, but he recreated his famous journey through Asia in the 1970s, *The Great Railway Bazaar*, in his 2006 book, *Ghost Train to the Eastern Star*. But why *not* recreate your own mythic journey, even if you're not so famous, even if you're not mythic . . . yet? A myth has to start somewhere. Perhaps you want to recreate that horrible trip you took with your mom and dad and your younger sister and brother to

Yosemite. Your mom and dad always wanted you to "See America," but all you wanted to see was the video screen playing *Chitty Chitty Bang Bang*, a movie your siblings hated, the source of many of your fights on that miserable holiday, culminating in your sister Becca grabbing the precious DVD from your sticky little hands and sailing the movie into the badlands of South Dakota. Some fun, huh?

Imagine if you recreated the trip, or some portion of it, what you might discover about your siblings and your aging parents. Of course, you'd want to avoid simple nostalgia on any such recreation because nostalgic and sentimental writing is usually pretty dishonest and selective. Nostalgia tends to reduce memory to some simple equation in which the past represents a simpler time and the present is complex and difficult, when in fact, if we're being honest, life is always complex and difficult, even for kids, sometimes especially so.

The Investigation or Forensic Journey

When is a search an investigation and when is it a quest? As in other areas, sometimes the categories blur a bit, but there are subtle differences between the two in travel writing. A quest doesn't have to be an investigation, and an investigation need not be a quest, which implies something approaching a life-changing experience. Any long-term project will change your life for better or worse, but in a quest you're actively seeking that change. In a forensic journey, you're most likely not seeking a life change as such. (*Forensic journey* is a term used by Eileen Pollack. In this case, I prefer it to the term *travel investigation*, so let's use that while crediting Pollack).

As I've mentioned, I've long been a traveler to the Philippines, and I'm no stranger to the hazards of that country, though these dangers are sometimes exaggerated by the Western press, and the country is often wrongly characterized as a lawless place full of would-be kidnappers and terrorists. I often tell people that no place in the world is safe, and that you might become the victim of a terrorist's bomb in Madrid, London, or Bangkok, as easily as in Manila. I tend to believe if your number is up, it's up, no matter where you're standing.

While I researched my book on the Tasaday, I was staying with my wife's family in her hometown of Kidapawan in Mindanao. At the time, the island, the second-largest in the Philippines, was going through one of its periodic and ongoing civil wars between the government and one of the Islamic separatist factions, in this case the Moro Islamic Liberation Front (MILF). One of my sources, with whom I'd had a bit of a falling out, Joey Lozano, a local journalist with ties to the communist and Muslim guerrillas in the area, wanted me to travel with him between the government and rebel lines to meet a key figure whom I had wanted to interview for quite some time. Margie and her family told me not to go. Not only did Margie distrust him, but her family thought the trip was too unsafe as well. After meeting with a well-connected Muslim woman named Taj Mahal, who told me that Lozano was bad news and not trusted by the Muslim fighters anymore, I decided to cancel my trip, much to the chagrin of the my would-be tour guide. I'm fairly certain that had I gone, he would have engineered my kidnapping or killing, because he knew by this point that my book was going to expose him for a fraud. The last time I'd gone anywhere with him, I'd wound up with an ArmaLite rifle pointed at my chest by a would-be kidnapper whom this same journalist/con man had hired to scare me out of the area (though I didn't know it at the time). As Filipinos often say, while shaking their heads, "Only in the Philippines."

At the risk of sounding cavalier, you get used to such things and quickly learn the Filipino mantra of *bahala na*, which is akin to the Spanish *que sera, será* (whatever will be, will be). I hardly ever visit Kidapawan without a bomb going off prior to my visit or directly afterward, having nothing to do with my visit and often nothing to do with politics as such. More often, the bombs go off in battles between local bus companies and as the result of personal vendettas. It's a country in which a few dollars can buy you an assassin. And the bombs are small ones, though they do damage. Once, after a bomb went off in the market, my father-in-law gave me a personal tour of the crater. I guess he saw it as a bonding moment between us.

It's unfair to characterize *all* of the Philippines in this manner. Such incidents happen more often in Mindanao by far than anywhere else in the country. But once Margie and I stayed for a few days at Dos Pal-mas, a luxury resort off the coast of Palawan. Nothing happened to us, except that we felt pampered and had a romantic getaway. A year later, the terrorist group known as Abu Sayyaf attacked this same resort and kidnapped the staff and guests, including three Americans. They be-headed one of the Americans almost right away. The other two were a missionary couple celebrating their wedding anniversary, Martin and Gracia Burnham. Abu Sayyaf kept the Burnhams in captivity for over a year, always on the run until Gracia was freed and Martin was killed in a botched rescue by the Philippine army. It could have happened to Margie and me, but it didn't.

I consider myself neither especially brave nor especially fearful. There are risks I'm willing to take and those that I'm not, and some risks that I don't even know I'm taking until I've taken them. But some writers will go anywhere for a story. Take, for instance, the unlikeli-est travel book of all, *The Tenth Parallel: Dispatches from the Fault Line Between Christianity and Islam*, by Eliza Griswold. In this book, Gris-wold makes my adventures seem like a stroll around the Epcot Cen-ter and redefines the phrase "off the beaten path" as she travels along the invisible line ten degrees above the equator to investigate the ugly battles between two major religions. Her investigation, in which she ventures to Nigeria, Sudan, Somalia, Indonesia, Malaysia, and the Phil-ippines is often more about the divvying up of scarce resources than the divvying up of souls. As the daughter of the former presiding bishop of the Episcopal Church, Griswold seems the perfect traveler and in-vestigator for the job. Along the way, she interviews Gracia Burnham and travels to Kidapawan, where my father-in-law doesn't give her a bomb-crater tour. She has more important rendezvous planned. Here, she meets with a Catholic priest named Peter Geremia, who lives un-der the constant threat of death from various factions. A month before her meeting with Father Geremia, two local journalists, married to one another, George and Maricel Vigo, were gunned down by a right-wing paramilitary group after meeting with Father Geremia. George Vigo was to have been Griswold's "fixer," a term journalists use for a local go-between. But Griswold hardly seems to need go-betweens as she follows leads that seem risky to the point of being foolhardy. In one memorable episode, she's invited to meet with a MILF commander with a hundred-thousand-dollar bounty on his head, who had narrowly escaped "a bloody battle with a local governor over a swath of potentially oil-rich swampland" (264). Unhappy that they were unable to kill the MILF leader, the government's thugs shot his wife dead instead while she was on her way to the mall for a shopping trip.

Accompanied by an entourage of the slain woman's female relatives, Griswold is ferried upriver in secrecy for several hours until she steps off at a spot where a hundred or more armed rebels greet her. Here she meets the rebel leader, whose hideout is an unused mosque, cooking himself a chicken dinner. The fighters at this rebel camp are all involved in justifiable *jihad*, she's told. The government has taken their land. When she asks for a show of hands to see how many of the people have lost land to the government, no one responds, so she repeats the question, thinking perhaps that something was lost in translation. Indeed, it was. She's informed that all the land the government took belonged to the MILF commander, twenty-five hundred acres in all. He used to be a wealthy landowner, and his private army consists of his serfs and relatives. Now that that's cleared up, he wonders if she might know of any American companies who'd like to prospect for oil or natural gas on the marshland he controls.

Only in the Philippines.

Obviously, such a book as this shares a lot in common with the investigative journalism we've previously explored. The reason I'd place this book in travel and my book *Invented Eden* in immersion journalism is simple. While place is important in my book, travel as such is not at its heart as it is in Griswold's. Her book explores not one place but many, and is held together by her rather brilliant observation that Christians and Muslims tend to clash along this particular latitude. She travels in pursuit of the question, *Why is that?*

The question of why or who or how or what is at the bottom of any investigation, but all forensic investigations are not necessarily so serious. Maybe you want to be the umpteenth person to investigate one of the perennial cable TV mysteries: the Loch Ness Monster, the Bermuda

Triangle, or Bigfoot. Good luck. Personally, that kind of forensic journey would bore me, partly because it's such well-worn territory. Unless
you have an uncle who's obsessed with Bigfoot and who wants to take
you on an expedition he's organizing. Then I'd say, absolutely, do it, because the investigation, if done well, will focus as much on your uncle's
obsession as whether or not Bigfoot is real. Such an adventure could be
great fun to read, though your uncle might never speak to you again.

But here's a thought: no matter how unserious a forensic journey
might seem at first, I will lay odds that by the end of your investigation, it will be deadly serious. Again, it's a matter of stakes. The time,
cost, and emotional turmoil caused by any investigation are guaranteed to make the stakes high for you. No matter what, you'll go places
you hadn't anticipated, you'll get more than you bargained for. And so
much the better. Otherwise, what's the point of writing? As the old saw
goes, "No surprise for the writer, no surprise for the reader."

Okay, but let's think of a really frivolous travel investigation. What
if, let's say, a bunch of rubber ducks fell off a container ship and you
decided to devote a couple of years of your life to what happened to
them? Actually, such an investigation would be pretty irresistible to me.
Unfortunately, the writer Donovan Hohn heard about it before I did.
In 1992, a shipment of 28,800 bath toys fell overboard from a container
ship during a fierce storm, and in the ensuing years, the toys by the hundreds washed up on the shores of Alaska and elsewhere and became the
stuff of legend.

With the birth of his first son imminent, Hohn sets off on an adventure to understand the odyssey taken by the nearly twenty-nine thousand bath toys (evenly divided between plastic duckies, beavers, turtles,
and frogs) from the toy factory in China where they were created to
the forlorn beaches on which they were found, and as a result writes a
fetching and informative book with an almost record-breaking subtitle,
*Moby Duck: The True Story of 28,800 Bath Toys Lost at Sea and of the
Beachcombers, Environmentalists, and Fools, Including the Author, Who
Went in Search of Them.*

Part of the joy of any investigation is meeting the eccentric people
who have devoted their lives to the very thing you're investigating. As

any good fiction writer knows, what happened is often less important than to whom it happened and why. This rule of thumb is no less true of the real life investigator. As your investigation progresses, the obsessions of those who came before you will undoubtedly rub off on you, coloring your own perceptions, driving you a little mad. In my case, the people who were most obsessed about the Tasaday hoax inquiry were the two journalists on either side of the story. In some ways, they became the story. The same could be said of the eccentric scientist in possession of Einstein's brain in Michael Paterniti's *Driving Mr. Albert*, and of course it's definitely true of the eponymous anti-hero of Susan Orlean's *The Orchid Thief*. Obsession breeds obsession, and that's as much what we look for in a narrative as the solution to our investigation.

In Hohn's case, the guru at whose feet he sits is Curtis Ebbesmeyer, the white-bearded, Hawaiian-shirt-bedecked editor of *Beachcomber's Alert!*, whose great passion and life's work is the study of ocean currents through the detritus discovered on shorelines around the world.

It doesn't take long for Hohn to become obsessed with the subject. Note in this passage how he approaches his investigation with the zeal of a religious convert.

> Sitting on his patio, I mentioned to Ebbesmeyer my dream of following the trail of toys from beginning to end.
>
> "It's an expensive thing to do the kind of traveling you want," he said.
>
> I told him I'd travel on a shoestring, roughing it, freeloading, hitchhiking, crewing on boats, whatever. I was convinced it could be done. Perhaps a shipping line would let me earn my passage to China as a cabin boy. Perhaps a magazine would send me to the Arctic on assignment. (44)

This investigation might sound a bit frivolous, but it's anything but that. While the book is ostensibly about a bunch of plastic bath toys that were lost at sea, it's really an investigation into the environmental degradation of our planet. Before long, we're learning about enormous "ghost nets" floating at sea and killing everything in their path, the breakdown of pelagic plastic, and dead zones in the ocean of a million square miles or more where the world's plastic sits and sits in a vat of plastic soup. The title and the nature of the investigation is a kind of lure, a bait-and-switch. You might think at first that you're in for a lark, but this investigation is as serious as that of *The Tenth Parallel*.

And that's all to the good. For any investigation to be worth the trouble for both reader and writer, it must morph and become more than you bargained for. It must be worthy of your obsession.

But, you might ask, who's going to pay for my obsession? The answer to that is simple, my friend. No one . . . most likely. Is a magazine going to pay for an expedition to the Arctic? Perhaps, but not if you're an untested writer. We'll learn more about the nature of a successful proposal soon enough, but for now I have to deliver the sobering news that most likely you're going to have to fund your own obsessive investigation and your own travel through massive credit-card debt and loans from indulgent relatives and friends. If you're going to go down, go down cheerfully. Don't simply court disaster. Marry it. You have to be a bit mad to be an immersion writer, so embrace your madness (though you might want to tone it down a bit if you're trying to mooch off of friends and indulgent relatives). Even if you're fortunate enough to land an assignment from a magazine, it's unlikely that you will be paid enough to make the trip worth it financially. Ask most writers how much they've made on their magazine pieces and they'll laugh ruefully. Either you want to investigate or you don't. If it's mostly the money that interests you, go for an MBA. If you're lured by the fame, go see a psychiatrist. The joy has to be in the hunt, in the process, more than in the reward. Not long ago, I signed a contract for a story with a well-respected magazine in which I traveled to three rainforests: in Ecuador, Omaha, Nebraska (it's an indoor rainforest!), and Australia. The editor said she could pay me eight hundred dollars. When I asked if she could throw in something for expenses, she hesitated and said, "Well, okay," and added an extra two hundred. Did I laugh in her face (this would have been difficult, though not impossible, as we were doing all this by e-mail and I would have needed to travel to laugh in her face)? No. I said *thank you*. I should add that in this case, I had already traveled to Ecuador and I had other funding for my trip to Australia. What I wanted to use the two hundred dollars for was my road trip from Iowa City to Omaha,

Nebraska, and even then I would lose money on the deal. I should also add that this magazine pays on publication, and my article took nearly two years to see print.

The Experiment

Okay, but what if you just want to have some fun? There's nothing wrong with that, is there? Does everything have to have the weight of the world and the fate of humanity hinging upon it? The cheery answer is, yes! Even if you believe that we're all doomed and you'd like to simply engage in some good old-fashioned escapism, it's unlikely that the universe will oblige you. As the old Jewish saying goes, "The surest way to make God laugh is to make a plan." It's hard to think of a sillier premise for a book than Julio Cortazar and his wife Carol Dunlop's *Autonauts of the Cosmoroute, A Timeless Voyage from Paris to Marseilles.* The famous Latin American novelist and his American-born wife had the idea to travel along the highway from Paris to Marseilles as a kind of voyage of discovery in 1978. Noticing how many rest stops or *aires* there were along the route, they formulated the whimsical idea of traveling the Autoroute at a snail's pace, actually examining it rather than rushing through it—the Autoroute as destination rather than as a means to a destination. With over seventy rest stops along the way, they planned to stop at two a day for a little over thirty days without ever leaving the highway. Along the way, two different sets of friends would replenish their stocks, but the couple would never leave the route themselves.

Unfortunately, Dunlop's health and then Cortazar's health postponed the trip, as did speaking engagements and the like, until finally in 1982 they decided that they could postpone the trip no longer. And so they embarked in their faithful vw minibus, named Fafner after a dragon in a Wagnerian opera, and made their slow perambulations southward. The book's dedication is worth quoting here, because it's one of the best ever written:

> We dedicate this expedition and its chronicle
> to all the world's nutcases

and especially to the English gentleman whose
name we do not recall and who in the eighteenth
century walked backwards from
London to Edinburgh singing
Anabaptist hymns.

Ah yes, what one person considers a fool's errand is to another a holy quest.

The book, for all its invention, still at its core has nothing less than love and death at stake. Dunlop, who was probably dying during the trip (though references to her ill health are veiled) didn't live to see her thirty-seventh birthday or the publication of the book. Cortazar joined her two years later. The Japanese view cherry blossoms just before the wind takes them away, believing that a thing is most beautiful just before its moment of departure, and it's this joyful and doomed exuberance that fills this wondrous book. What starts out as a complete lark of an experiment eventually takes on an undeniable beauty as the travelers' imaginations take flight and they start to notice the loveliness of . . . yes, the rest stops, or more accurately, the notion of resting and stopping and noticing. What takes them over a month to complete could normally be completed in a long day's drive by most travelers, and at the end of it, they find themselves wistful and disappointed to rejoin the rushed pace of society, not glad at all that it's behind them.

> Sadness: that's what there was. A sadness that began two days before the arrival, when at the Senas rest area we looked each other in the eye and for the first time fully accepted that the next day we would enter the final stage. How can I forget Osita [his nickname for Carol] saying: "Oh, Julio, how quickly the trip went by . . ." How can I forget that at the moment we read the sign announcing the end of the autoroute we were so filled with anguish we could only combat it with an obstinate silence, which accompanied us till we entered the clamour of Marseille, looked for an empty spot in the Vieux Port and put our feet on land that was no longer Paris-to-Marseilles land. A triumph clouded by tears we dried in a café, drinking the first *pastis* and thinking that this very afternoon we would drive up to Serre for a few days' rest. (347)

It's best for such experiments to seem at first glance to be larks, but only at first glance. If the stakes aren't high, you won't be able to sustain the idea. If you don't see your voyage as a voyage of discovery, no matter how frivolous or absurd it sounds, your readers will find nothing to discover either. Cortazar and Dunlop's book is all the more moving because of their openness to this process of discovery. Essentially, the book is a love story, though an unconventional one, told in not-strictly-alternating chapters between the pair. In the end, when they're safely back in Paris and have revealed to their friends the nature of their journey (which they had kept a secret to all but the few people who helped replenish their supplies along the way), their friends are delighted and amused and ask if their "intentions had been simply playful or if behind them lurked a different sort of search, the *immersion* [emphasis mine] in a landscape not merely geographical, the confrontation with ordinary life and with the defiant no-man's-land established in the middle of the frantic pace of civilization" (351).

Cortazar and Dunlop are dazzled and amused by their friends' interpretations of their intentions, but they admit that no, these were not their intentions. Perhaps these were their unstated intentions, subconscious intentions, but the trip is all the more wondrous and moving because their intentions, if that's what they truly were, are discovered at the end of the journey and not at the beginning. Foremost, Cortazar writes, they discovered a "month outside of time, that interior month where we knew for the first and last time what absolute happiness was" (351–52)

Cortazar and Dunlop never thought of their voyage as a mere stunt. If you think of your writing as a stunt, as my desperate narrator does in the poem I wrote, "Rejected Book Ideas," then everyone else will regard it as a stunt, too. But the writing of the more substantive lark-with-stakes journey has a long and glorious history—it certainly didn't begin or end with Cortazar and Dunlop.

In the late eighteenth century, Frenchman Xavier de Maistre was placed under house arrest for engaging in a duel. While imprisoned for forty-two days, he decided to explore his confines, and the result was the delightful travel book *A Journey around My Room*. The book is written in a satirical fashion, parodying in many ways the great voyages of discovery by noted explorers. He travels north and south in his room and views paintings and furniture as though encountering them in a distant land:

> My room is situated on the forty-fifth degree of latitude, according to the measurements of Fr. Beccaria; it stretches from east to west; it forms a long rectangle, thirty-six paces in circumference if you hug the wall. My journey will, however, measure much more than this as I will be crossing it frequently lengthwise, or else diagonally, without any rule or method.—I will even follow a zigzag path, and I will trace out every possible geometrical trajectory if need be. I don't like people who have their itineraries and ideas so clearly sorted out that they say, "Today I'll make three visits, I'll write four letters, and I'll finish that book I started."—My soul is so open to every kind of idea, taste, and sentiment; it so avidly receives everything that presents itself. . . [suspension points from original] And why would it turn down the pleasures that are scattered along life's difficult path? They are so few and far between, so thin on the ground, that you'd need to be mad not to stop, and even turn away from your path, and pick up all of those that lie within your reach. (7)

The writer who tackles a travel experiment sallies forth to do battle with drudgery, routine, and boredom by taking a second look at the everyday through the injection of whimsy and chance. Unlike a scientific experiment, over which control and at least a notion of the desired results preside, the travel experiment thrives on its very unpredictability, the thrill of not knowing what you will discover. In *Truckin' With Sam*, Lee Gutkind's son stuck a pin blindly into a map to determine each summer where the father and son would venture. In William Least Heat-Moon's *Riverhorse*, the author tried to make his way across the United States by boat even if in spots he and his companions had to occasionally carry the craft between bodies of water.

In most cases, the limitations or restrictions of your travel experiment are essentially the organizing principle or conceit of the project. What you do with this conceit will either make or break the essay or book. Restrictions or limitations seem to me the lifeblood of the travel experiment. In the case of Dunlop and Cortazar, they restricted themselves to two rest stops per day. They would travel to the first after breakfast and stay there until lunch. At the second rest stop they would spend the night, no matter how ugly or inconvenient the site was. William Least Heat-Moon restricted himself to travel by boat. Lee Gutkind went anywhere the pin stuck. De Maistre could travel no farther than his room. Almost invariably, the restrictions, which at first seem so confining, achieve the opposite effect—when confronted with restrictions, the human mind overcomes them by force of imagination.

In De Maistre's case, he wrote his *Journey* as a lark to alleviate his boredom, but his brother liked it and had the volume published, and to Maistre's surprise, he became something of a literary sensation. But even De Maistre, at the end of his confinement, felt wistful at its completion because he had taken the time to transform his incarceration into an opportunity to observe his world more closely, the mark for which all such experiments should aim.

Exercises

1. It's getting more and more difficult to find a good journey to reenact, but I don't think the one mentioned by Cortazar and Dunlop has been taken: the gentleman who walked backwards from London to Edinburgh. It's yours for the taking! But if that doesn't trip your trigger, then try reenacting a trip from your own past. In my case, I'd probably choose to reenact my only long-haul hitchhiking experience, when at the age of twenty-two, I traveled from Bloomington, Indiana, to Iowa City with my friend J. V. and his dog Pook (the Wonder Dog) to check out the place before I started graduate school. Along the way, we were picked up by a stripper named Jimmie Day and a World War II vet from Casper, Wyoming, named Miles Carter, who claimed to have been a fighter pilot with General Chennault's Flying Tigers. Obviously, the trip was an important one for me. Sadly, Pook has shed this canine coil and J. V. and I have lost touch, but now, over thirty years later, I live

in Iowa City after a twenty-something-year absence. The obvious path of reenactment would be to do the trip in reverse, from Iowa City to Bloomington, maybe in part to reconnect with my old friend and the sense of self I left behind. What great or not-so-great trip would you choose to re-enact?

2. In *Heathrow Diary*, Alain de Botton spent a week at Heathrow Airport gaining access to a behind-the-scenes look in a place most of us want to hurry through as fast as possible on our way to somewhere else. Take a page from de Botton and spend a week camped out somewhere we usually avoid, say, a graveyard or in a mall (obviously, the logistics of this are half the battle—getting permission, first of all). But even if you can't spend a week in an unusual locale, brainstorm between five and ten such places that might be worth infiltrating. Which of these places seems most promising to you for a project. Why?

3. Writer Eileen Pollack uses a helpful term for the travel investigation: she calls it the *forensic journey*. Whatever you call it, the world is full of mysteries and riddles worth solving. I've always been interested in the Sphinx's nose, which was reputedly shot off by one of Napoleon's soldiers. A cursory glance at the Internet shows that this story is, however, not undisputed, and various alternate theories abound, each one loaded with various cultural and political baggage. Ah, so much the better to investigate. My essay, "Who Gave the Sphinx a Nose Job?" would take me to Cairo, of course, because nothing can beat actually seeing, touching, and smelling (especially where noses are concerned) a place, and who knows what characters I'd run into with their own crazy and wonderful theories about the Sphinx's missing nose? Of course, travel takes money and time, and it's not always possible to find either in great quantity. So if you can't actually travel to Egypt or its equivalent, then do a little brainstorming. List five mysteries big or small you'd like to investigate. Sasquatch? The Bermuda Triangle? Nah. Those are too easy. You can do better than that.

4. A quest can be sublime or ridiculous. Eric Weiner went in search of the happiest places on earth in *The Geography of Bliss*. My next quest

or pilgrimage will be to the birthplace of C. M. Coolidge. *The* C. M. Coolidge, that master of schlock who in 1903 was commissioned by a cigar company to paint sixteen images of dogs playing poker. Cassius Marcellus Coolidge was born to abolitionist Quaker parents in Antwerp, New York. That's where I'll be headed, and I'm also going to try to view in person all sixteen famous images. I doubt I can track them all down, but I'll find a few most likely, and part of the story will be, of course: who owns these paintings? Laugh if you must, but two of these paintings sold at auction a few years back for $590,000. In the end, I'll visit Coolidge's grave in true pilgrim style. Perhaps I'll look for a holy relic, too. A petrified chew toy in the shape of a beer bottle, perhaps?

5. If you were going to set off on a journey with limitations, what would those limitations be? How would you avoid the "Rejected Book Ideas" syndrome, a gimmicky approach such as traveling via baby carriage that would prove nothing except how silly you are? You probably don't want that as your literary legacy, do you? "Oh, right, the baby carriage guy."

6. Pretend you're Herodotus and take a little trip: you can visit a nearby town or city or state. Interview several people about their local customs and beliefs. Ask what makes their place special and if there are any miraculous sites that would impress a visitor from a far-off land. Try to play it as straight as you can (if you dare). The results should be fun if you can capture the right tone, the right sense of wonder and/or awe. Try to capture the tone of Herodotus, separating what you can verify with your own eyes from hearsay.

Chapter Four

Ethical and Legal Considerations

M ost writers I know live somewhere between dread and denial when it comes to legal matters and ethics. I'm no exception. With both *Invented Eden* and *Do-Over*, I worried throughout the writing process that someone might be angry with the results and sue me. *Invented Eden* was quite a public story, and the people whom I knew would be angry with the book were journalists and a couple of anthropologists.

I felt pretty sure that one of the journalists, a Filipino reporter based in Mindanao named Joey Lozano, had arranged the kidnapping of a rival group of reporters from Germany's *Stern Magazine*. They had come into the Tasaday rainforest on the heels of Lozano and Oswald Iten, before Iten broke the hoax story in 1986. Meeting their guide in the forest on the way back from the Tasaday caves, Lozano quizzed the guide, the original "discoverer" of the group, the hunter Dafal, who had been sent to replenish supplies.

While Dafal was off on a supply run, the pair of *Stern* reporters were being treated to a stone-age farce at the caves. But the ruse was so unsophisticated as to be laughable. Locals were showing up by the dozens claiming to be Tasaday and dressed in whatever leafy garb they could find, including one man who decided to cross-dress in a leaf brassiere. If the mastermind of the so-called hoax, Manuel Elizalde, was behind this deception at the caves, he was doing it from afar, from his self-imposed exile in Costa Rica. But sure, I can see him shouting into the phone from Costa Rica, his message relayed by shortwave radio, "Don't forget the leaves!"

More likely, the people at the caves were motivated by a desire to be fed. *If we pretend to be Tasaday and dress up in leaves, we're going to get things.* Completely logical. If I were one of them, I'd do the same, I'm sure. Many years later, I experienced locals siphoning off my supplies, as well, and people tagging along to be fed. I had to have my supplies replenished, too.

The day after Lozano met Dafal, the *Stern* reporters were kidnapped and held for ransom by a shadowy group of ex-soldiers, a "lost command," as they were known. But in the fluid political landscape of Mindanao, they could have been anyone. Lozano knew all these people well, as I found out on a later expedition in 1999.

On my own trip, when we were close to the Tasaday reserve, we stopped in the mountain village of a chief Lozano knew, Datu Galang. Lozano sent for a couple of Tasaday to meet us in the village. This was the same place where he and Oswald Iten had met the Tasaday in 1986, when they supposedly told Iten (with Datu Galang and Lozano translating) that the whole Tasaday discovery had been a hoax, that they were simple farmers who had been coerced into playing dress up. But when two Tasaday men eventually showed up, they were accompanied by a group of men armed with ArmaLite rifles, who held me at gunpoint for the next several hours, though I was allowed to briefly interview the two Tasaday men. Right after that we hightailed it out of the place on horseback, hopefully never to return, as far as Lozano was concerned. But I did return six months later, with a group from the other side, and we met the same Tasaday men, who each separately and out of earshot of the other told me that when they had been sent to meet me they had been told that their old friend and benefactor, reporter John Nance, wanted to see them and when they'd met me, a stranger, they were disappointed.

Who were the armed men? I asked. They were the men of Datu Galang, not Tasaday guards posted by the hoax makers to keep curious visitors such as myself out, as I'd been told by Lozano. In other words, they were employed by our hosts, and Lozano's negotiations with them (away from my view) were obviously a sham. I taped all of this, both meetings actually, and I had the translations independently verified. I had been set up by Lozano.

Later, after reading correspondence from Lozano to Iten, it became clear to me that Lozano had also set up the *Stern* reporters to be kidnapped (though without Iten's knowledge). But I couldn't prove it. My evidence was circumstantial, and so I framed it in the book as a possibility, a suspicion. Then I waited for the fallout.

Of the hoax proponents, I heard only from Lozano, who sent me a sneering e-mail. Iten reportedly threw my book against the wall when he read it. The other major hoax proponent, Judith Moses, an ABC producer who was as zealous about the Tasaday being a hoax as John Nance was about them being "authentic," died before the book was published. I surely would have heard an earful from her had she lived, but I strongly doubt she would have sued me. She was a journalist, first and foremost, and believed in free speech, and in any case, the only person whom I had perhaps besmirched was Lozano. Not long after the book was published, he, too, became gravely ill and died. I never would have wished for this, of course, but their deaths raise an important point. The dead can't sue for libel.

Actually, libel laws do vary from country to country, and so it's best to check your local laws. In China, relatives of the dead *can* sue for defamation, and in the Philippines, libel is a criminal act, and you can be jailed if someone brings a libel suit against you. In the Philippines, it's often cheaper and more expedient to simply have someone who's libeled you shot (though not advisable all the same).

Now would be a good time to take a look at what constitutes libel in the U.S. But before we go any further, let me make a caveat: I'm not a lawyer. For specific legal advice, you should consult a lawyer experienced in these matters. A good place to start might be with Volunteer Lawyers for the Arts (http://www.vlany.org/aboutus/index.php). Amy Cook has written an excellent article on this subject for *Writer's Digest*, which is available online: "A Writer's Guide to Defamation of Character and Invasion of Privacy" (http://www.writersdigest.com/article/defamation-and-invasion/). For more on this, I might also recommend (ahem) my own book *Turning Life into Fiction*, which deals with these questions from a fiction writer's point of view.

Basically, libel is the written dissemination of falsehoods about another person that damage his/her reputation and/or business, or unfounded attacks on that person's character. Okay, get ready. Here come some bullet points:

- The best defense you have against a defamation lawsuit is that your book is well researched and you can back up all of your claims as fact.
- The second best defense you have is that such legal cases are expensive to mount and damages awarded tend to be small.
- Don't state your personal opinion as fact. Make it clear that it's your opinion and that it's based on something real. When I wrote of my suspicions that Joey Lozano had something to do with the kidnapping of the German journalists, I put it this way: "The tantalizing question is not whether Dafal or Mai Tuan arranged to have the *Stern* team kidnapped but whether Lozano had anything to do with it." I didn't say he had, but I raised the possibility. If I had written, "My hunch is that Joey Lozano arranged for the *Stern* reporters to be kidnapped," I probably would have been okay, too, given his later behavior toward me, the circumstantial evidence I had, and the lies he told me. But if I'd written, "Joey Lozano undoubtedly had those reporters kidnapped," this would have been a potentially libelous statement.

Invasion of privacy is another matter. If you're writing about a public figure, he/she probably can't win a lawsuit against you. Public figures, for the most part, give up their right to privacy where the written word is concerned, at least (though not necessarily the right to privacy of their children or spouses or other relatives).

When you're dealing with private individuals, the question is as much about ethics as it is about the law. We'll deal more with this in a bit, but I always ask myself if what I'm revealing about someone else is relevant to the story and if it reveals something about the other person that might have negative repercussions in his/her life. Augusten Burroughs, author of *Running with Scissors*, was sued by his former foster family for defamation and invasion of privacy, and Susanna Kaysen was sued by a former boyfriend for suggesting in her book *The Camera My*

Mother Gave Me that he had sexually assaulted her. Kaysen won her case and Burroughs settled out of court. Regardless, a lawsuit takes a toll emotionally and financially, whatever the outcome.

The litmus test for such cases is whether the disclosures you make are in the public interest, in which case the first amendment protects you. But what does "the public interest" mean? As with all such notions, it's open to interpretation. The fact that a publisher has published your book demonstrates a certain amount of public interest. Likewise, if the events involve yourself, as they did in Kaysen's example, the court is more likely to give you broader protection under the first amendment. If, however, you're writing from a journalist's perspective, you might have less protection if you "out," say, a rehabilitated felon whose crime was committed twenty years ago and who has ever since lived a model life.

I once sat on a panel at a book fair in Seattle with true-crime author Ann Rule, the writer who rose to fame with her 1980 memoir/biography *The Stranger Beside Me*, about serial murderer Ted Bundy. I can sometimes be blissfully ignorant of entire subcultures and true crime is one of these, so I had no idea who this nice older woman was who looked like one of my grandmother's canasta buddies. I was the only person in the room who didn't know who she was, and it soon became apparent that no one was all that interested in what I had to say to the packed room. They wanted to hear what Ann Rule had to say. Me, too.

She told us all cheerfully that her latest serial killer subject was filing lawsuit after lawsuit against her, and she was just as cheerfully batting them away. "Happens all the time," she said. "He has all the time in the world to file as many lawsuits as he wants."

Most of us aren't as blithe about such things as Ann Rule, or as wealthy, and so the threat of a lawsuit, frivolous or not, is enough to send a chill across our writing projects. Anyone can sue for anything, and even a frivolous lawsuit can cost time and money to have dismissed.

When you sign a book contract, you should pay special attention to the indemnity clause. Have an agent or lawyer take a close look at it for you. Any legitimate publisher carries media liability insurance to protect them against lawsuits. But that doesn't let you off the hook. While your publisher might well mount a defense if you're sued, it might be written into your contract that you split the legal costs. Let's say that legal fees mount to a hundred thousand dollars or more. Your share is fifty thousand. What's worse is that if they settle, you might be forced to settle as well. Most publishers want to avoid a lengthy court battle and so they'll often cave in, and let's say they decide to settle for one hundred thousand. Guess what your share will be? And that's without your say-so.

The good news is that you, too, can purchase media liability insurance, and you probably should if you have any worries at all about potential lawsuits. Again, you'll need to pay close attention to the deductible and exactly what's covered and for how long. Several organizations offer such coverage to their members and you should consider joining one of these groups, not only for this, but also because they provide other valuable services to writers. The policies are pretty affordable, especially considering the alternative, but again, make sure you know exactly what you're paying for. In the U.S., the organizations that have agreements with insurers for their members include:

The Authors Guild (http://www.authorsguild.org/)
National Federation of Press Women (http://www.nfpw.org/)
The National Writers Union (http://www.nwu.org/)

Of course, it's best to avoid defaming someone in the first place, and so I tend to proceed with caution if I'm concerned at all about liability. When I was writing *Do-Over*, I worried about the people into whose lives I was entering, and when necessary I changed various things about them to protect their privacy. I changed the name of anyone under eighteen, and while I always received permission in writing from the various school districts and even the parents of children whose classrooms I was attending for a week at a time, I was still cautious about revealing too much about the teachers in these classrooms. Before the book was published, I gave a reading from it at Vermont College of Fine Arts. When it was over, my friend Larry Sutin, a fellow author and a former lawyer, approached me and suggested that I should remove a passage from the book that one of the people I had written about might find embarrassing and slightly invasive. Unfortunately, it was a really funny moment in the book, and it wasn't all *that* invasive, but I didn't want to worry about it—and worry I would have—so I followed Larry's advice and removed the passage.

Throughout the process, my editor assured me that the book would be *vetted* by the publisher's lawyers. To vet a manuscript is to analyze it legally. In theory, the lawyers are supposed to flag whatever might be potentially litigious and then quiz you about these things, and it was a process I both looked forward to and dreaded. When the day arrived and I spoke with the lawyer, I was surprised by how little he had flagged. He wanted me to change one detail, something I *never* would have thought potentially libelous. I had mentioned that a boy had been expelled from my old boarding school the day after I arrived in 1974 for using heroin. I had mentioned the boy's first name. That was it. And thirty-five years had passed. Couldn't I just take out the name? Nope. The lawyer wanted the passage removed. Then he asked me if there was anything else that might be cause for potential concern. Wasn't that *his* job? Had he even read the book?

Still, I felt relieved that there seemed to be nothing actionable in the book, or very little, but I also felt alone and more vulnerable than I would have wished.

Here's a bit of a paradox. I don't actually believe there *is* anything actionable in the book. Even so, that doesn't make me worry any less when a book comes out. I know too many horror stories.

What happened to British author Martin Goodman is a prime example.

In the 1990s Goodman researched and wrote an authorized biography of Indian holy woman Mother Meera, *In Search of the Divine Mother*. The book, which he terms a "quest/biography" placed him in the midst of her devotees as a fellow traveler. He said to me, "The immersive part was writing from that devotional space while bringing in a heightened critical and investigative awareness. It's a part of my mode of entering different cultural experiences and reporting back for readers" (interview with author, December 28, 2010). He was given access to her devotees, her family, and even guided through her home village in India by family and devotees. The family told him stories they weren't supposed to tell, and "the investigative part" of him took over. Not that the resulting book was an exposé, but it portrayed Mother Meera's origins as a poor servant girl. Her followers believe her to be a god, and as Goodman stated in an interview with me, "Gods don't have human stories."

When Mother Meera read the book in manuscript form, her assistant met with Goodman and told him he must destroy the manuscript. It was Mother Meera's request. The rejection stung and Goodman argued for a while, but this reaction to what he considered a largely favorable portrait of Mother Meera essentially killed the book for him. Part of the argument for chucking the manuscript was that divine truth is so far beyond human truth that his task was deemed hopeless by Mother Meera and her inner circle. The devotee part of him listened to what they had to say and agreed to destroy the manuscript while the investigative writer part took their opinion as a challenge. He destroyed the manuscript and all its copies, even wiping out the digital copies on his hard drive. Still, he told Mother Meera's assistant that he reserved the right to take another stab at the book at a future date, and to retain his notes.

That future date arrived sooner than Mother Meera and her followers probably expected. He wrote the book again, a different, angrier sixty-thousand-word version that he pounded out in two weeks. Then he threw out that version, too.

Once again, he wrote another version and sent it to his publisher. This was the version they accepted.

When the time came for him to correct the final galley proofs, he went through the manuscript one last time to take out any phrases still tinged by anger, then packaged the book for shipping. Afterward, he checked his e-mail and found an intimidating message from Mother Meera's husband. His reaction? He opened the package back up and reinstated the angry phrases he had cut.

The threat of litigation, as I've mentioned, is often as effective (probably more effective) as litigation itself. Galleys of the book had been sent out to various reviewers, and after a publicist who was a follower of Mother Meera's received a copy, Goodman's publisher, HarperCollins, received a threatening letter from a high-powered attorney, also a follower of Mother Meera's. On the day of publication, Goodman was called into a meeting at HarperCollins headquarters in New York with the publisher's lawyers and questioned. His answers, he felt, didn't matter. It wasn't the fear of losing that worried them, but the fear of litigation itself and the enormous cost of fighting a legal battle. They decided to cancel publication of the book and pull all the reviews. They even forbade him to read from his book.

But one scheduled reading went ahead, and with his books sealed in boxes like contraband in a back room, he read to a packed and appreciative audience at Lenox Hill Bookstore on the Upper East Side of Manhattan. His launch party also went ahead at a friend's home.

Unknown to him at the time, an employee of HarperCollins had attended the reading incognito (HarperCollins employees were forbidden to attend), and the next day when he checked in with the publisher, they had done a complete about-face. Now they declared they weren't going to succumb to bullying! Publication of the book would proceed after all.

A litigation lawyer went through the manuscript again and found nothing that should be changed. Everything finally seemed set, but the publisher still kept stalling for weeks. Clearly, a little nudge was needed. This same publisher had recently caved in to China's bullying to suppress a memoir by Chris Patten, the last British colonial governor of Hong Kong before the 1997 handover from Britain back to China. One day, Goodman called and left a message for the general counsel of HarperCollins. With all the negative press over Rupert Murdoch (who owned HarperCollins) bowing to Chinese pressure to kill Patten's memoir, Goodman figured he was sitting on a great journalistic story of his own . . .

Five minutes later he received a return call from the general counsel, and publication proceeded quickly from that point on.

Sadly, the accrued damage had been considerable due to the delays and HarperCollins's craven actions. They had already pulled the reviews of the book, and those reviews weren't returning. The publisher Roger Straus once wrote in a letter to my father that every book has its "*moment juste*," the right time for publication, and clearly, the *moment juste* for this book had passed. Paperback plans were cancelled and the book was remaindered within six months.

Despite the heartbreak for the writer inherent in such a story, Goodman considers the publication of the book a victory. Of course, we want our books to reach as wide an audience as possible, but often this is up to the whims of people who couldn't care less about a book's merits. If you become obsessed with a project, as you should, the doing of it should count as much as its reception, because the reception of any book is outside of your control. As Goodman said to me during an interview,

> [*In Search of the Divine Mother*] became one of those do or die books, a writer standing up for what he sees to be the truth. So yes, there was no future without it. In literary terms, the book is a unique contribution to knowledge so I am proud of that. I don't know of any other book that got under the wire to tell the story of a major religious figure before the myths were established. The myths were being established, but I was able to find the more regular tales from which larger ones were elaborated. It was like being given the chance to write one of the Gospels. A task like that is bound to land you in trouble, I suppose; it has to be contentious. But the book is one of real value, it is as accurate as I could make it and still tells an inspiring story, so I'm glad.

Note that Goodman's biography was neither a hagiography (a reverential biography) nor an exposé. Goodman tried to achieve balance, and of course that's what upset his subject so much. "When a biographical subject threatens litigation maybe you have the balance about right," Goodman says. When I first started writing *Invented Eden*, I received a similar bit of fair warning. Another writer of nonfiction told me, "If both sides hate your book, you'll know you've succeeded." I'd say that's true. You shouldn't write to please someone else, though of course you should aim to write fairly and accurately. In my case, the hoax side hated my book, and the authenticity side had its quibbles, too. Most importantly, always keep your notes! They will be an excellent defense if someone comes gunning for you. The fact that someone is offended by what you've written about them doesn't mean that they have any kind of a legal case against you. Some people need to be offended. If what you've written is accurate, if you're not reporting hearsay as truth, if you're not affecting someone's employment by transmitting falsehoods (i.e., "Everyone knows that so-and-so is a pedophile,"), then you're probably protected. Not completely protected, alas, as we've seen, because complete protection against a lawsuit is something like achieving Nirvana, but protected enough in most cases.

Goodman's story is an extreme case, but not unique. And unfortunately, there's simply no way to predict what the reactions of others will be in all cases to what you've written. If you're writing a blog, the same standards apply. Still, while there have been some major punitive awards given to litigants who were the victims of defamation on the Internet, there haven't been quite as many as you might expect. On the Internet, people tend to fight free speech with more of the same. There's certainly no shortage of false information and aspersions of character on the Internet, but reactions here tend to resemble a verbal barroom brawl. If you're going to take part, you wade into the crowd, fists flying, while ducking out of the way of flying chairs. Likewise, misinformation can be easily corrected on the Internet in a way that hard print can't equal, as it can't be so easily changed.

Ethics

I'm not trying to terrify you, really. In nearly thirty years as a writer, I can think of few people I know who have been sued or threatened by a lawsuit, and I know a lot of writers. Unless they're not talking about it. But I've never been sued either, or threatened with a lawsuit (I'm looking for a big chunk of wood now) though I have lost friends as a result of what I've written. Ironically, I suppose, the friends I've lost were as a result of short stories I'd written in which I'd based a character on someone real, not pieces of nonfiction.

When you write about someone else, you should remember and not take lightly that you have all the power in this relationship, at least until you're sued. You will often affect someone's life in a way they might not like, but they might not tell you directly and instead may simply drift away from you.

If you're uncertain about their reaction, you have four choices. Get ready. More bullets:

- *Change aspects of their identity.* When I was working on *Do-Over*, I changed the names of anyone under eighteen, except for my own children, and I changed the names and identifying characteristics of other people I encountered, to protect their privacy. If I was at all uncertain, I changed what I could without going too far into the realm of fabrication. Some periodicals will not allow you to do this—for instance, the *New York Times* has a policy of *not* changing names, which can get awkward, as it did for me when I wrote a piece about the end of my first marriage for the *Modern Love* column. I was able to simply refer to "my wife" in the column. You should note that changing identifying aspects of a person doesn't necessarily protect you from a lawsuit. It can help but it's not foolproof.

- *Show your subject what you've written about her or him.* This is a gamble. Some writers show everything to their subjects and get their approval, but many don't. As a rule, I don't do this because it encourages self-censorship (I'd better not write this or so-and-so will be angry. You don't actually know if so-and-so will be angry, and even if they are, that alone shouldn't necessarily be the determining factor).

- *Compose a waiver for your subject to sign.* This is an iffy proposition, and one that I've never tried and don't intend to try. Personally, it would scare me if someone approached me and said, "I'm going to be writing about you. Will you please sign this waiver promising not to sue me?" At the very least, I'd want some kind of approval over what was written about me, wouldn't you? For me, this approach is too compromising to the writer. You can write about me without such a waiver as long as you don't spread

malicious lies. Fact checking, of course, is a good thing, and
journalists have written things about me that were untrue, but
not out of malice. They had simply failed to check their facts.

- *Do nothing and cross your fingers.* This is actually the most common approach. Don't write anything false that might defame
someone. Respect the privacy of others as much as possible
without compromising your book or essay and you'll most likely
be okay. But if you're concerned, take out media liability insurance *before* you publish the book. And be honest with your publisher's lawyers. Better you address a potential problem before it
becomes a real problem.

Writing about Family and Friends

We all do it. This is the most fraught territory for most writers. As I
mentioned, I've lost friends over what I've written, I'm sad to report.
I should add, too, that my friends were better than what I'd written
about them. Generally speaking, we're not afraid of being sued by our
relatives, but of being ostracized by them. Unfortunately, this is territory you'll have to cross on your own. However you approach it is
right for you, but most families have a stake in protecting the Family
Myth of Perfection. Even mine. When I wrote my book about my sister, my mother, also a writer, was terribly nervous about the book and
wanted me to turn it into a novel. She constantly asked me what I was
writing, and so I struck a deal with her. I'd show her the book *after* I
had finished it. I didn't want her input before then. In the interval, my
mother developed severe glaucoma and macular degeneration and was
unable to read the book when I had completed it. So, in order to fulfill
my promise to her I had to go to her apartment every night and read
a chapter of the book to her. As you might imagine, this was quite difficult, but I had to do it. At one point, I stopped at a passage I knew she
wouldn't like at all. It concerned the night of my father's death and my
mother's reaction as reported by a good friend who had been with her.
The scene was excruciating in its portrait of her denial, but it was also a
sympathetic rendering, I thought. Still, I knew that I could simply skip

over the passage and spare us both some pain. But I couldn't. I took a deep breath and pushed on. After I read it, my mother was quiet and I asked her how she felt. We talked about it for quite a while, and though I can't say she loved the passage, we talked honestly and openly about my father's death in way that we hadn't before then. But I'm not fooling myself. She let me keep the passage because she loved me, no other reason. I'm sure she hated it.

Other kinds of reactions are possible. For example, an aunt of one of my friends was so scandalized by her memoir that she threatened to picket the hometown bookstore where my friend was scheduled to do a book signing. Of course, my friend was delighted. You can't buy such great publicity. Sadly, the aunt didn't follow through on her threat.

In the age of the Internet, you should assume that your most far-flung relative, friend, or enemy will know about and have access to anything you write about them. Sure, you can assume a nom de plume, a pseudonym, but that won't guarantee anything. A friend of mine changed her name for a memoir she wrote, afraid that her parents would be upset. When the book was published, she received a great review in the *New York Times*, which also published her photo alongside the review. Her parents, avid readers of the *Times*, opened the paper that Sunday and . . .

When I wrote about my own children in *Do-Over*, I tried to be as careful as possible with their feelings, aware, too, that none of them were really old enough to give me informed consent. My kids at the time were three, twelve, and sixteen. There were a couple of passages that could have potentially been embarrassing for my older daughters, one in which my daughter Olivia (who, along with her sister Isabel, are from my first marriage) first said she was going on a trip to England with us over Thanksgiving break, and then decided not to go so she could be in the school play—after I'd purchased nonrefundable tickets. I didn't portray her as a brat (she's anything but that). This was simply a moment of conflict we had and it caused me some pain, the least of it financial. I think sometimes we do ourselves and others a disservice when we pretend there's no conflict between people who love each other. If I had presented my children in this way, they would have simply been cardboard cutouts. That doesn't mean that everything I wrote about them stayed. On the contrary, my editor, a good and kind soul with kids of his own, urged me not to include another passage that I might have regretted later. He was right and I took that passage out.

Writing about Others

Unless you simply don't care about the effect your words might have on others, you really should give some consideration to this, especially to those we might call the innocent bystanders of your tale.

One of the reenactments I wanted to do for *Do-Over* was to live again for a few days in one of my childhood homes. Imagine receiving a request from a stranger to live with you for a few days. I didn't know who was currently living in my old homes (there were about five) so I had to address my letters to "Occupant." Not very promising, I know. I overcame this in part by writing my letter explaining my project on University of Iowa stationery, and including a business card as well as a copy of the article I'd done for *New York Magazine*. Then I sent the little package via FedEx. Most people are going to open a package sent FedEx, I believed. And then I waited for a response. A week went by and I received a tentative e-mail from the current resident of one of my childhood homes. She said she was willing to entertain the possibility of my project, but she had a lot of questions. After a couple of e-mail exchanges she stopped responding, and I never heard back from her again, though I'm fairly certain my e-mails to her were respectful and professional. The thought of opening her home to a stranger must have been a little too creepy for her, and I can't say that I blame her. Who knows? Maybe someone else in her family—her husband or one of her children—objected.

After another several months went by, I figured I wasn't going to get the chance to complete this do-over. But then I heard from another homeowner. This was from a house I lived in as a teen in South Bend, Indiana, where my mother had been a professor at Indiana University South Bend. The occupant of my old home was also a professor, but at Notre Dame, and after thinking it over, she said she'd be willing to

ETHICAL AND LEGAL CONSIDERATIONS   161

participate for the sake of professional collegiality if I was willing to accept a couple of conditions. "I don't want to sign up to be an incidental character in your adventure," she told me, an entirely reasonable sentiment, I thought. It's good for writers to be reminded of this from time to time. People don't exist simply to populate our books. Sounds obvious, but not everyone wants to be an incidental character in our adventures, and there should be some opportunity for them to opt out when possible. So I agreed to hide her identity. I didn't state her address and I changed a few identifying characteristics of the house. I gave her a new name and changed some other aspects of her life as well, and I revealed nothing of her private life. I also gave her the opportunity to see the chapter I had written about the experience before I even showed it to my editor. As a result, she corrected a few factual errors I had made, but not much else. In a couple of instances, the small changes I made to protect her identity confused her a bit. I had changed the color of her house from white to yellow, and she noticed this and wondered if the 'mistake' had been intentional or not. But she said she liked the chapter. The experience was completely pleasant for both of us. She was doing me a favor by letting me into her life, and I wanted to return the favor by respecting her wishes. I should note that none of the changes I made tipped this chapter into the realm of fantasy. It's not at all uncommon for nonfiction writers to alter small identifying details for the same reasons I did.

Throughout this book, I've mentioned the matter of trust. When you enter into people's lives as a writer, you're asking them to trust you, to be unguarded, to come clean and reveal things they might not otherwise share with anyone. I've met many writers who are happy (or at least fully willing) to betray this trust. In *The Journalist and the Murderer*, Janet Malcolm opens by writing, "Every journalist who is not too stupid or too full of himself to notice what is going on knows what he does is morally indefensible. He is a kind of confidence man, preying on people's vanity, ignorance, or loneliness, gaining their trust and betraying them without remorse" (3). She goes on to state that the subject of a profile feels especially betrayed because the writer who had previously appeared so friendly, so interested in the subject's view of the world, really had no intention of telling the story the subject wanted told. The journalist is always in it for himself. "There is a splinter of ice in the heart of the writer," Graham Greene famously observed (quoted in "Ways of Escape," The Economist, September 30, 2004, http://www .economist.com/node/3242458). And Truman Capote, toward the end of his life, pouted about his friends deserting him because he had revealed all their secrets in print, as William Todd Schultz discusses in *Tiny Terror*: "I can't understand why everybody's so upset. What do they think they had around them, a court jester? They had a writer" (10). Certainly, there's a *caveat emptor* aspect to writing. Unless someone is paying you for a hagiography, chances are they're not going to be pleased with the results. When I wrote my piece on summer camp for *New York*, one of the owners of the camp kept following me around nervously, realizing perhaps too late what she had done. I tried to be honest. I told her that she probably wouldn't love everything I wrote about the camp. "Why not?" she asked. "Why don't we aim for that?"

"Because I'm not writing a brochure," I told her.

So, yes, writers can be bastards, okay? Guilty as charged. But we also have to acknowledge that subjects can be unrealistic in what they expect of writers. If someone knows you're writing about them, it's partly their problem if they expect you to write a completely laudatory article, a puff piece. It's not necessarily your job to protect them.

The trust issue depends on your relationship with the subject and what you've promised or led him/her to believe. Remember that a number of the authors I've discussed here decided early on that they were going to be trustworthy about some aspects of their projects, though not necessarily all. Kevin Roose didn't tell anyone at Liberty he planned to write a book, but he also decided early on that he wouldn't lie about who he was or where he came from. The same held true for John Howard Griffin. Bill Buford in *Among the Thugs* seemed rather pleased that his thuggish friends trusted him—I'm not criticizing, but his subtext seems to be, "Sucker!" when he writes of the first soccer fan he befriended, "That was the thing: He trusted me."

Your own conscience has to be the guide in this—there's an obvious problem with an immersion project if you divulge too much. If the root of your project is in itself a deception (as it was in the case of both Roose and Griffin) you can't waste too much time on feelings of guilt, or else why bother? And the deceptions themselves are not immoral, but ultimately pretty respectful. Neither Roose nor Griffin were pretending to be, say, Holocaust survivors so they could get sympathy. They weren't writing fake memoirs such as the one by the white guy who pretended to be a Native American author named Nasdiij, or the several fake holocaust memoirs, such as Benjamin Wilkomirski's *Fragments*. They were taking on these other identities for the purpose of learning something they couldn't have learned otherwise, not to live permanently in those identities until being unmasked.

On the other hand, what of someone such as Joe Mackall, who wrote about his Amish neighbors? One of the reasons Mackall's book is so lovely is due to the respect he obviously shows his neighbor, Samuel, and the respect Samuel has for him. It's only right and proper that he gave Samuel the opportunity to look at the book and comment on it before it went to press. Mackall remarks, in an e-mail to me:

> Samuel and Mary read the book at the same time my Beacon editor read it. I had this arrangement with Samuel and with Beacon. To its credit, Beacon wanted Samuel to read the book early on, almost as much as I did. I met with Samuel and Mary at their kitchen table and we went over things. Samuel had a list of things he wanted to talk about. Most of these were just little things I'd gotten wrong: "That hog was 350 pounds not 250." That kind of thing. At one point he said, "I think I told you too much." The only thing he said he wished would not appear in the book were a couple of things he said about his brother-in-law that were a bit critical of him. I had no problem taking these two instances out of the book. Besides that, he asked for no other changes. I'd built up over ten years of trust by the time I wrote the book, so we were both comfortable talking about anything . . . So far there has been no fallout for Samuel and we're still good friends. I'm not the kind of writer who can drop subjects from his life once I've written about them. I think it makes

for a better book and a more honorable profession if we—subject and writer—realize we're in this thing together, even if, as we know, the subject has a lot more to lose. (January 7, 2011)

Still, even the most sympathetic writer can inadvertently change the lives of the people he or she writes about, sometimes for the worse. Gerald Durrell, author of the wildly popular memoir *My Family and Other Animals*, about his idyllic childhood on the Greek island of Corfu, felt enormous guilt over his role in bringing hordes of tourists to Corfu, contributing to ruining what had been to him a natural paradise.

And when James Agee visited the sharecroppers of Alabama in 1936, he was a wholly sympathetic observer in their lives, but his trip with Walker Evans had repercussions well past Agee's death. During his time with the sharecroppers, he became especially close to a smart ten-year old named Maggie Louise. Her favorite book, as Agee noted, was a geography text from third grade, *Around the World with Children*, but until Agee and Evans showed up, she was only dimly aware that every child in other locales didn't suffer as she did, her hands rubbed raw and bleeding in the monotonous rhythm that was her life in the fields every summer. Dale Maharidge writes:

> Agee filled Maggie Louise's head with exciting ideas, things she had never thought possible. He stretched and challenged her intellect, and as Maggie Louise came to like him more—after taking rides all over the county with him in his automobile, so much more exciting than her father's mule-drawn wagon—she began to wonder about the outside world, questioning whether there was more to life than cotton farming.
>
> One night, Maggie Louise and Agee were sitting on the porch, her sister Gretchen later recalled from stories Maggie Louise told. The two rose to walk in the darkness among the chicory weeds growing in the packed earth behind the house. He lifted and perched her on the roof of the chicken coop that stood to his shoulders, her legs dangling over the planks, white and cracked as beached driftwood, so that she was looking down at him as they talked. Maggie Louise always spoke fondly of that moment to her sister. She looked down at this man who knew so many things outside their county and asked him about eternity, the stars

in the heavens. It was one of those clear Alabama nights, a sky weighing on them as if they were suspended at the bottom of a black ocean, the bright shimmerings of the Milky Way floating on the surface. Crickets and the call of distant whippoorwills were the only voices besides theirs. Maggie Louise questioned many things. Agee tried to explain. She wondered about her future. He later wrote she might get her wish and become a nurse or a teacher, getting away from this life. He told her about city life in New York, and it all seemed wonderful.

Maggie Louise was full of expectations. Her grades were among the best in her school. Her parents supported her. It seemed the possibilities were as vast as the sky.

In the years that followed, she'd recall that night to friends. She'd speak warmly of Agee. He had confirmed for her that the world was bigger than Alabama cotton. She liked what he had said. (iii)

After Agee left that summer of 1936, Maggie Louise's dreams of a bigger world receded like a dust cloud behind Agee's car. She never became a nurse or a teacher, never left the fields. As Maharidge writes, with each passing year, she "went from great expectations to hopes," and then those hopes faded, too. Thirty-five years after Agee's visit, she bought rat poison at a store and drank it. As her family and doctors tried to save her life, she fought them, ripping tubes from her arms and refusing saltwater her sister tried to give her to force her to vomit. She screamed at the doctors and told them she didn't want to live, that she'd had enough, and her last words right before she died were, "Tell Mama I'm happy now" (v). She was buried a couple of miles from the chicken coop where she and Agee had dreamed.

When Maharidge returned to revisit the story in 1986, some of the people he encountered were bitter and didn't want to speak to him. Word of Agee's book had trickled back and a few thought they should have received some money (though Agee never received any royalties). Although fifty years had passed since Agee's visit, it was well remembered, and one of the people who had been a young man when Agee visited took one look at Maharidge and remarked bitterly, "You're back."

Of course, we can't blame Agee for any of this, nor does Maharidge. Nor, as far as we can tell, would Maggie Louise have done so. And who's to say what else in her life contributed to her decision to end it? Still, hers is a powerful story, and should be a caution that when you enter into someone's life your actions have consequences, no matter how compassionate you are. I'm not saying you should take responsibility for every reaction to what you say or write, but for you to simply be mindful. That's enough.

There's another way of looking at this, of course. There's indeed something positive to be gleaned from Maggie Louise's story. Without diminishing the tragedy of her life, let's just say that her story has affected a great number of people, first in the portrait Agee wrote of her as a smart and curious ten-year-old who was also the victim of a feudal system that ruined lives by the thousands. She was not the victim of Agee or Maharidge; on the contrary, Maharidge and Agee honored her by writing about her. And this is indeed the flip side that we must keep in mind as writers. By and large, the writers I know are not manipulative and selfish, but are among the most generous-spirited people on the planet. When you immerse yourself in someone else's life, more often than not you're enshrining them, not using them. Most writers earn little if anything from their efforts, except for the satisfaction of telling and retelling the complex and myriad stories of humanity, of which theirs, too, are a vital and necessary part.

Exercises

1. Interview a friend whose life and/or views of life you find intriguing, troubling, and/or unusual. Your job is to pry, but gently. You want to show by your friendly smile and your relaxed posture that you're the subject's friend, and that he or she can trust you. Take notes but don't use a voice recorder. It's good to do more than one interview of your subject, ideally three or so over several weeks if you can afford it. Ask some of the same questions over again and notice how over time your subject becomes more comfortable with you. When you feel you have

sufficient information about your friend, identify where you think the story lies. It's often in the details that your friend might not like to have written. But go ahead. Remember, this is just an exercise. It's not for publication. After you've completed your interviews, write your sketch and leave nothing potentially embarrassing out. When you're finished, write a one- to two-page reflection on your own sense of ethics regarding this assignment. Do you think your friend would be hurt or embarrassed by what you've written? Are the things you've written fair? How would you feel if these things were divulged about you? Do you like your friend more than what you've written? Would you show it to her? Would you edit it based on her concerns?

2. Do the same exercise, but with a family member. How are the results different from the portrait of your friend? Did you self-censor more or less? Do you feel you have more of an agenda in writing about your family member? Is it fair?

3. Do the same exercise, but with a stranger. The same questions apply. Is there anything actionable in what you've written? If you published the piece, do you think a court might say it serves the public interest?

Chapter Five

Legwork

The Proposal

When I first considered writing a book about the Tasaday hoax controversy, I needed to write a proposal. By no means do all books, articles, or essays need proposals. As David Shields said to me not long ago, "Many of the books you and I love would have made no sense as a proposal." And he's certainly right. There are few if any editors who would have jumped at Geoff Dyer's book *Out of Sheer Rage* before it was written. Now he's well known enough that a proposal for this book might fly, but at the time it would have sounded absurd to most publishers: *I plan to write a book about trying to write a book about D. H. Lawrence.*

But some books depend on proposals to be written. As publishers are in the business of selling books, they want to put their money behind books they think will sell to as many people as possible. The first thing you need to consider is whether or not your idea is suitable for a proposal. Here are brief descriptions of two books I've written: "I'm going to write a book about a 'tribe' in the Philippines that was discovered in 1971 and hailed as the 'ethnographic Find of the Century,' only to be derided fifteen years later as one of the biggest hoaxes of the century." And, "I'm going to write a book about my older sister Nola, who was a diagnosed schizophrenic and who died of a prescription-drug overdose when she was twenty-five." As a reader, the second idea might well appeal to you more than the first, but the concept of the first would catch a publisher's attention much more readily than the second. The second book was undoubtedly dearer to my heart than the first, though I spent twice as much time on the Tasaday book as I did on my book about my sister. I knew going into my book about my sister that a proposal would have seemed ridiculous—if it was going to be written, I would have to write it for no other reason than I wanted to write it. Likewise, my book *Nola* was a reflective memoir, not an immersion memoir, and so it simply demanded that I sit in my chair every day and write, while the Tasaday book would demand many interviews with authorities on the subject the world over. In order to cover my travel expenses and to sound credible enough to secure those interviews, I needed to sell it to a publisher.

I came to the story of the Tasaday with no strong preconceptions except the hunch, based on the flimsy news accounts I'd read, that they were most likely a hoax. This open-mindedness was probably the single most important factor that allowed me to gain access to almost everyone involved. I was not an anthropologist, though I'd studied anthropology in college. I was not a journalist, per se. I was not the friend of anyone involved.

Still, I was by no means a Tasaday expert. I didn't even have much of a track record as a nonfiction writer. At the time, I had published five books, and only the book about my sister could be truly considered a work of nonfiction (I had also written a craft book, but this was concerned with fiction). So I had a fair amount of convincing to do. I should say that in this case, the help of my agent, Jennifer Hengen, was invaluable. She was able to arrange a conversation with an editor who was intrigued by the idea. We chatted for an hour or so and then the editor told me to spend the summer writing a proposal. One of the crucial aspects upon which the success of my proposal hinged was my access to experts on the subject. I didn't know any Tasaday experts. So I entered *Tasaday* in my pre-Google Web browser, and a name appeared: John Bodley.

At the time, I lived in Bellingham, Washington, and Professor Bodley also lived in Washington. He taught over the mountains at Washington State University in Pullman. I quickly dashed off an e-mail to Professor Bodley and asked him if he would be willing to chat with me about the hoax controversy. Almost immediately I heard back that yes, he'd be happy to talk with me about the Tasaday. I had no idea at the time how fortunate this first encounter was for me, as John Bodley was one of the few people involved with the controversy who took a middle-of-the-road position. Both sides of the highly polarized camps respected him. He had participated in a hastily called conference on the Tasaday controversy only a few months after the initial hoax story broke, held at the University of the Philippines. The author of a widely used text, *Victims of Progress*, Bodley is a well-known anthropologist, and while he wasn't a Philippines expert (his fieldwork had been conducted in South America), his human-rights advocacy made him especially appealing to the organizers of the conference. The emotional register of this time in the Philippines was high pitched, even shrill. The Tasaday had been declared a hoax only a couple of weeks after the fall of the hated Marcos regime to the People Power Revolution, and the organizers of the UP conference saw the gathering as an opportunity to pound another nail into the political coffin of Ferdinand Marcos. The Tasaday had been something of a showcase, a PR bonanza for the regime in the early years, and now it was widely believed that a poor group of farmers had been coerced into playing cave people for the benefit of this corrupt regime. In other words, any real sense of scientific inquiry was in short supply at the conference. Bodley and fellow anthropological experts were supposed to venture down to Mindanao to meet the so-called Tasaday for themselves after the conference, but that never happened because the situation was deemed too unstable. Or so they were told.

He had left the conference intrigued, but by no means convinced either way.

Meeting him was like attending Anthropology Boot Camp. He was kind enough to put me up at his house and devote an entire weekend to my edification. I wasn't completely ignorant about anthropology. I'd been keenly interested in it from high school onward and had briefly majored in it in college. But there was a lot to digest. I spent much of the weekend copying his files, which he opened up completely to me, and more importantly, he challenged some of the terms people casually throw about when they're discussing indigenous peoples. What did we mean, he asked, when we used such words and phrases as *isolation, Lost Tribe, authentic,* and even *hoax*? These early discussions were of great importance to me and framed much of the way I approached the story from that point on, with an appreciation of the ambiguities in the story and the various agendas of the many players.

Of equal importance, Bodley opened doors for me. My visit to Bodley did not go unnoticed in Tasaday-watcher circles. Once I'd spent time with him, he was able to vouch that I was reasonably intelligent and that I did my homework. Still, at first, both sides were suspicious of me, and several of the people to whom I wrote replied as though they thought I was an agent from the opposing side of the controversy. The sides had been pretty well staked out for years, and they didn't trust strangers. So I took what I call the *village-idiot approach,* which wasn't far from the truth. In the village-idiot approach, you admit to the person you want to interview that you know nothing or very little. Enlighten me, you say. That doesn't mean that you should actually *be* an idiot. If you want to be a true village idiot, then you'll need to consult *The Complete Idiot's Guide to Immersion Writing,* not this book. The village-idiot approach merely entails an open mind, but does not exclude in any way you doing your homework. Before you meet with anyone you want to interview, you should read up as much on the subject as possible, and you should know as much about the person you're interviewing as possible. There's no excuse for laziness, and you will only annoy and alienate the expert to whom you're talking if you ask him or her the most basic questions. You'll definitely start off wrong if you ask, "So can you tell me what your work is about?" I've been asked that question several times by lazy interviewers and it doesn't make me enthusiastic. On the contrary, it makes me feel disrespected by someone who couldn't even bother to enter my name in a search engine.

The village-idiot approach is not dishonest, or at least I didn't see it as such when I was working on my Tasaday project. You're simply acknowledging to the person you're interviewing that he/she is an expert while you're not. When some of the people I wanted to chat with were resistant at first, I simply appealed to their greater knowledge (and sometimes their greater egos!) in the area. "Well, I'll be writing about the subject anyway," I'd say. "It would be so much better if you gave me your side of the story, because I haven't made up my mind yet." And I hadn't. In fact, I thought it was strange that nearly everyone required me to make up my mind and reach a conclusion before I had conducted my investigation. It's fine to have a hunch, but to go into an investigation knowing your conclusion already seems disingenuous. Around the time I was first conducting my research, I ran into a reporter for the *Los Angeles Times* who had become cynical and embittered by just such imperatives in his profession. When he was the bureau chief in Atlanta for his paper, he had gotten in trouble for sending reporters to investigate stories with an open mind. An open mind costs too much money, his boss told him. You have to choose the angle first and then investigate. In other words, the reporters had to have their minds made up and simply confirm the angle from which they approached the story with evidence that supported it. As I mentioned earlier, that's called *confirmation bias* and we're all susceptible to it, but it seems wholly unethical to embrace your bias while foisting your investigation off on an unsuspecting public as "objective."

There are no strict guidelines for a proposal in terms of length. A proposal for a magazine story should only be a couple of pages in length and should give the editor a sense of your prose style. Think of it as an audition. For a magazine, it's not a bad idea to have several ideas to pitch to an editor. It's also a *very* good idea to know the magazine to which you're pitching. The more familiar you are with a magazine's editorial slant, the more likely you'll pitch an idea that's appropriate. Developing a book proposal is another matter entirely. A good book proposal can take a considerable amount of time and energy to develop; often, months of preliminary research are involved. A sample chapter might also be required, and is in any case a good idea. Certainly, there have been book proposals of only a page, but these are quite rare. I hesitate to state an average page length, but twenty-five to fifty pages is probably the norm (including a sample chapter), and there have been a number of proposals that have gone over a hundred pages. My proposal for *Do-Over* was only about ten pages, but my agent sent out the proposal the week after my article on returning to summer camp appeared in *New*

York Magazine. Timing, in this case, was on my side. My proposal for
Invented Eden was twenty-four pages. This is how it began:

Invented Eden

THE MAKING OF A STONE AGE TRIBE

Sometime in the '60's, or maybe it was the 50's, or maybe a time before
that, before history, a hunter named Dafal, from the Manobo Blit tribe
wandered deeper into the forest primeval of Mindanao, a southern island of the Philippines, and stumbled upon a people we did not know
existed, nor did they know of our existence. At first, the people were shy,
and ran from him whenever he approached, but little by little he coaxed
them out of their natural reticence. He left them gifts, pieces of cloth
and brass, earrings and little tools. And with every gift he gave them,
he made them less of what they were and more of what we are. He gave
them things they did not have names for, and they were curious, and
they wanted more, and he wanted them to leave their jungle, to meet his
friends, people he said who would look after them.

When he found them, they wore nothing but leaves, and they lived
near a mountain they called Tasaday. They foraged for roots and the occasional frog, tiny fish, or crab caught in a stream. They knew nothing
of agriculture, and their basic tool was a scraper, a stone used to scrape
pith and shape bamboo into knives. Sometimes they ate monkey meat,
but this was a delicacy. They had lived there longer than anyone could
remember, and the only other people they knew of were two groups
who lived like them, the Tasafeng and the Sanduka, with whom they
intermarried. But no one had seen the Tasafeng or the Sanduka for a
long long time, and now there were no more women to marry.

They had a legend. And in this legend, a great man came to them,
Momo Dakel Diwata Tasaday, Great God of the Tasaday, a man their
ancestors had told them about, and he did good things for them . . .

* * *

In May of 1997, Manuel Elizalde, a Harvard-educated Filipino indus-
trialist and a Marcos government minister, died at the age of 60. With

him died perhaps the definitive answers to what might have been the greatest scientific hoax of all time, the discovery of a Stone Age tribe, the gentle Tasaday who lived in the jungles of Mindanao. In 1971, Elizalde announced to the world the discovery of the Tasaday by the hunter Dafal, and the astounded world, both scientific and lay, bought the story almost without question. Fed by a media blitz that saw one film crew after another traipsing into the jungle, the Tasaday became Stone Age celebrities, as though Fred and Wilma had returned in a kind of Second Coming, and the world saw a chance to return with them to a romanticized Stone Age paradise.

Elizalde kept tight control over the Tasaday, allowing visitors in to see them in short helicopter forays. President Marcos immediately declared the 45,000 acres of jungle around the Tasaday a reserve for them, and Elizalde claimed that his control over the reserve was necessary to protect the Tasaday from the evil influences of the outside world.

What I attempted here was to quickly contextualize the story for the reader, while also giving a sense of the stakes involved and a taste of my prose style.

The first thing you'll want to write is a three to four page summary of your project with which to lead off. The more certain you are of yourself, the more convincing the proposal will sound to publishers. The aim of the proposal is to convince the publisher to buy your book. How many words do you expect the book to be? Eighty thousand? A hundred and twenty thousand? Books are expensive to print and a publisher will want to know that you have a target for the length of the book. Those three to four pages will also give an editor a good idea of your style. And marketers. Unfortunately for authors, there are fewer and fewer editorially driven publishing houses in existence. What this means is that even though an editor might love your proposal, if the marketers can't figure out how to sell such a book, it doesn't matter how much the editor loves it. They're not going to make an offer on it. Even though it's the job of the marketers to sell your book, more and more of the burden of marketing books is falling on the hapless author. And when a book fails to reach a wide audience, who is inevitably blamed?

The author, of course. The marketers and editors will take a step back. *Do I know you?* And it will be all the more difficult to sell your next book because the sales figures on your old book will come back to haunt you. But let's put aside that ugly reality for the time being.

In Proposal World, you're confident and self-assured. You're full of potential and there's nothing in the world more promising than the book you're going to write. After your summary, you will probably want to follow up with a short section on the research that will be required for the book. This is where you show that you're the right writer for the job. What are your qualifications for writing the book? Who are your John Bodleys? Do you have access to experts? What about sources such as archives and letters, diaries, anything that shows you're serious and you will be taken seriously by others? Do you have some good quotes from experts? They don't necessarily have to be quotes they've given you. They can be from secondary source material, articles you've already read on the subject. The main point is to show that you're informed. How much time will be needed to conduct the research? Where will the research take you and how will you arrange the time to conduct it?

After the section on research, you'll need to follow this up with another section on audience/marketing/promotion. The publisher will want to know how savvy you are about the audience for your book, and how you will help with the book's promotion after the book is finished. If you're an immersion writer, it's likely you're not shy, so that helps. Of course, promotion means a lot more now than it used to mean. In the old days, an author went on a book tour, but publishers do not love these, and it's only authors who sometimes still see them as glamorous—but many authors who've read to crowds of two or three people don't find them too glamorous, either. Promotion now involves blogging and using all the social media at your disposal. But also keep in mind the natural constituency for your project. Let the publisher know what connections you have to any group that might find the book naturally of interest. While book tours are pretty much déclassé, book clubs are a different matter entirely. Assignment to a book club guarantees that its members will each buy a copy of your book, and if you can demonstrate that your book would be of interest to such groups, so much the better.

Following this, you should include a chapter-by-chapter synopsis of the book. If you envision the book having fifteen chapters, then you should write summaries of each of at least three or four paragraphs. Don't worry. Your book will inevitably change. Most publishers understand this and won't hold you to every detail in the proposal. On page twenty-three of my Tasaday proposal, I included the following paragraph, which, in retrospect, strikes me as goofy, if not entirely insane:

> I plan to attach myself to a group that is already going to the area, though my fantasy would be to invite key members of the controversy on the same Tasaday expedition. For me, this is a kind of Everest expedition, like Jon Krakauer's *Into Thin Air*, though hopefully not with such dire consequences. I'd love to invite various players in the saga to go with me: Iten [Oswald Iten, the reporter who broke the hoax story] and Nance [John Nance, who wrote the book *The Gentle Tasaday* and whose journalism career was ruined by the hoax scandal] (who seem to hate one another, or at least feel mutual disdain). But that's certainly not necessary to the book.

Actually, maybe the idea wasn't *quite* so goofy as all that. John Nance had himself proposed the idea to Iten, I later found out. Of course, Nance had everything to gain and Iten had nothing to gain and was also fearful for his life if he returned to the Philippines while Elizalde was alive, and so he refused. The conventional wisdom by the time I reached the story was that the Tasaday were a bald-faced hoax, which was Iten's position. Admitting he was wrong (which he was) would have served no purpose. I later met them both and I did indeed go to the area with proponents from both sides, but on separate occasions and funded solely by me. The idea that there might be groups going to the area to whom I might attach myself was naive, though I'd assert mine was a necessary naïveté. You can't know in advance everything that you'll encounter or discover in this kind of book. As long as it's not a completely implausible idea, you should feel free to strategize. Happily, I included a caveat mentioning that my idea was "not necessary to the book." Above all, this group-travel idea showed my determination and enthusiasm, which never really wavered, though I experienced many days of frustration.

You're still not done with the proposal.

Now you need to write a section on the book's competitors. Have there been any other books like yours, and if so, what are they? Give a brief synopsis of each and include in what ways they're similar, but more importantly, how your book will add something new while at the same time appealing to the audience already created by this other book. Remember, you're speaking to book people. Don't try to bluff them. You should truly be familiar with the books about which you're writing.

Finally, wrap it up with an about-the-author section, and then of course your sample chapter.

Okay, now you're ready to present your proposal. If you need an image to sustain you from this point forward, think of a Roman galley slave. Imagine a cruel Roman soldier standing above you, his red cape flapping in the wind. You say you're exhausted? Don't see land? You're thirsty? You'd like some sleep, maybe even some payment? He raises his whip and laughs. "You can sleep when you're dead," he says. "Here's your payment," and he cracks the whip. How's that for encouragement?

But okay, I'll lighten up. A little. True, you're the slave, but you're also the Roman soldier. You've got to crack the whip. No one else is going to do it for you.

Had I known what was going to be involved in my Tasaday project at the proposal stage, I might not have gone through with it. I remember it now as a bit of a nightmare: five years of research and writing. Sure, the trips all over the world were stimulating, bracing, and sometimes terrifying. I visited the Tasaday twice, was held at gunpoint during one of my visits, took a trip to Switzerland and stayed with the reporter who broke the original hoax story. My original sense of what the book would take to write was so far off the mark it's laughable now, and I think maybe after all I *was* a bit of a village idiot, in that regard at least. I thought that I'd only need to pop over to the Philippines for a couple of weeks, but my first visit was nine weeks and didn't begin to cover all the bases I needed to cover. I also told my editor the book would take two and a half years, but that wasn't even close. Publishers of course want you to take as little time as possible, and while nearly all publishers will grant you an extension or two, it's best to frontload a little extra time into your proposal if possible (an extra six months or a year). There's often a big difference between when you would *like* to turn in your book and when you really can deliver. Here, I should also state unequivocally that I'm a big, fat hypocrite. I often use a deadline as a spur so that I won't procrastinate. I set my deadline for *this* book, for instance, absurdly early and yes, I had to ask the publisher for an extension (imagine a little throat clearing and a cough or two, followed by an awkward pause at this point in the book).

My advance for *Invented Eden* seemed sufficient when I signed the contract, but most advances are divided into thirds: a third paid upon signing, a third paid upon delivery and acceptance of the manuscript, and a third upon publication. In my case and the case of many authors, the entire advance and more was spent well before the book saw publication. Still, would I consider the project worth it? Yes, I have no regrets. The project was the opportunity and adventure of a lifetime.

Magazine Proposals

If you're writing a proposal for an article rather than a book, all this obviously needs to be scaled down considerably. A page or two is a good size for a proposal. My proposal for "Big Man On Camp" for *New York Magazine* was an e-mail to one of the editors, followed by a phone call once the editor expressed interest. The magazine proposals I've written that have been successful have most often involved a couple of pages of text, followed by a conversation with the editor. In most cases, the editor is not working alone, but in turn must pitch your idea to a meeting of other editors. Considering the limited space that most magazines have, even good ideas mostly get nixed at these meetings, and only a handful are given the green light. I try to have four or five ideas that I can pitch to a particular magazine so that if one gets shot down, I'll have another to take its place. The most common reason I know of for a magazine to turn down an idea is that "we've already got something like that in the works" or "we published something like that last year." Well, maybe that's true, but remember, this excuse is exactly what *O Magazine* told Melissa Pritchard about her Afghanistan idea. She went ahead and wrote it anyway, and then eventually sold it to *O*.

One more bit of advice on the proposal: the more you've thought through the idea, the better. Don't write, "I've always been intrigued by Bigfoot and wonder if he's real." You can substitute nearly anything for "Bigfoot." The more open-ended your idea is, the less likely a magazine will be interested. You might not know the end result of your piece, but you should at least have an intriguing angle. An editor at a major magazine once told me that one secret of writing a good proposal (for his magazine at least) was to take an angle that's anti-intuitive. By example, he told me of a proposal he had accepted about the historic Hatteras Lighthouse in North Carolina, which was in imminent danger, because of erosion, of falling into the sea. Millions of dollars were being mustered to move the lighthouse further inland, but this author presented the anti-intuitive alternate to this proposal. Instead of saving the lighthouse, the author asserted, we should let the sea take it. Without a doubt, this is a much more intriguing idea for an article: why we should let the Hatteras Lighthouse fall into the sea. That's an article I want to read. Not that the article changed things. The lighthouse was indeed moved and saved, at least for the time being. But that makes the article and its argument no less interesting.

A Few Words on the Interview

Inevitably, in an immersion project, you'll be conducting interviews. One of those little pocket-sized recorders will make you feel like a real writer, but they're not always practical and they make people nervous. In some cases you need to use them to protect yourself and to protect others, but in those cases you should ask beforehand if the subject minds being recorded. Let them know why you're recording and what the recording will be used for. If they say no, you have to respect that.

Sometimes they will say yes but ask you to turn off the recorder so they can say something off the record. If you want to get the best interview possible, you'll need to make the subject relax and trust you (even if they shouldn't trust you!).

My preferred method of conducting interviews is to have a recorder running but to take notes in my notebook. This forces me to pay attention, and the things that I choose to write down tend to be the juiciest quotes. If I rely entirely on a recorder, then I'm making my work much harder. I will then need to type transcripts of the interview at some point, or pay someone to do this. Transcription is a long and tedious process. I like to use the recorder for verification, nothing more.

Please don't be the interviewer who asks the subject basic questions that you should already know. Do your homework first and learn everything you can about the subject before you conduct the interview. You will impress your subject all the more if you've read some of what she's written (if she's a writer), have viewed his visual art (if he's an artist), or have familiarized yourself with her scientific studies (if she's a scientist). There are so many bad interviewers out there that a good one will seem like a friend. Your subject will be inclined to like and trust you and will feel more inspired to open up.

You should also listen to yourself. See what kind of interviewer you are. When I interviewed my mother for my memoir about my sister, I was horrified when I played back the first tapes and heard that I was doing most of the talking. A good interview can indeed be a conversation, but give your subject room. Quite often you simply need to stand back and listen and gently prompt rather than prod the person you're interviewing.

If you're able, interview your subject on several occasions in different locales. Maybe conduct one interview in the subject's home, another at a coffee shop, another in a different location. Repeat yourself from one session to the next. Don't ask all identical questions, but sometimes asking the same question twice can yield different results. This method will establish a priceless rapport between you and your subject. The first time you interview someone you don't know, you're a stranger. By the third time, you're at least an acquaintance, if not a friend. This, of course, raises all those thorny ethical issues once again, and if you need absolution, you won't find it here. If you need a refresher, take another look at the previous chapter.

The Proposal Reconsidered

Let me state something that is obvious but nonetheless often overlooked: having a book contract is not the same as having a book.

Someone might well buy your proposal, but you still have to write the book. Ask yourself whether you really need to sell the book before it's been written. There are advantages in having a proposal and advantages in not having one. At its crassest level, having a book contract is an ego boost. Someone thinks your idea is good. Hurrah! Now get to work. Someone thinks you're good enough to write the book. Huzzah! Now get to work. Someone paid you real money to write the book. Yay! Now get to work. Sadly, there's always real work involved.

Truly, if you can afford to write the book without a contract, this is not a bad way to go. First, you can write the book on your own terms. Once it's done, then you can shop it around. Once you're locked into a contract, your options are narrowed considerably. Suddenly, you have an audience of one, your editor. If your concept of the book doesn't jibe finally with your editor's, he or she might not accept the final version of the manuscript, or else might force you to change it so completely that it doesn't feel like your book anymore. You also have to consider that editors move around quite a lot. It's not only possible, but it's likely that the editor who acquired your book will not be the same one who ends up with it. It can be quite scary having a book "orphaned" at a publishing house. If your original editor leaves or is fired, the book will be assigned to another editor, and in many cases that editor will not have a lot at stake in the publication of your book. I've known of many an orphaned book that died on the vine simply because it was assigned to an editor who had no investment in it. In many ways, having such an experience is worse than not publishing the book at all, because authors are judged on their books' track records. If the book does not do well, who will wind up looking bad? Not the editors.

While I've been fortunate in having editors who cared about my books, I'll tell you this: half my books have been written under contract, and with each one of those books, the editor with whom I finished was not the editor with whom I started. In one case, I went through three editors. No matter the result, it's nerve-wracking and at times disheartening.

And think about this, too: big advances are not as common as they used to be. If you're fortunate enough to get a big advance, your troubles have just begun. Now you have to earn it back. If you don't, then don't expect a warm reception for your next book proposal.

I'll state it again: some of the best books would have made no sense as proposals. A book such as *Let Us Now Praise Famous Men*, by Agee and Evans, *did* admittedly begin as an assignment from a magazine, but it morphed so completely in the actual *doing* of the book that it never appeared in the magazine that assigned the piece, and only barely appeared in print at first, selling a mere four-hundred copies during James Agee's lifetime. Now it's rightly considered a classic (and it's one of my favorite books), and thank God James Agee wrote the book he wanted to write and not the book he assumed would sell. It was terribly taxing on him, but it's a gift to the rest of us.

My second editor for *Invented Eden* once told me that he doesn't buy books that are based on someone going out and having an experience and then writing about it (books not like *Invented Eden* but like *Do-Over*). Obviously, he wasn't the editor for *Do-Over* (and was long-gone from the publishing house where he had been my editor by the time I pitched *Do-Over*). But someone else obviously *was* that type of editor. My point is that if you want to write the book, if the idea is compelling enough, it comes down to finding the right editor who is in love with the idea and your writing. Joan Didion has said that if no one paid her for her writing she wouldn't write. Luckily, there have been plenty of people willing to pay for her writing. But that's not the case for most writers. When I wrote my memoir *Nola*, I wrote it without a contract and I hardly showed it to a soul until it was near completion. I didn't want anyone else to interfere with the book as it developed in my mind, a long, delicate, and risky project. When it was complete, two publishers wanted to buy it: one was a small, respected press that loved the book as I had written it, and the other was a major press that wanted me to turn the book into a more conventional memoir. I chose the smaller press because I wanted this book to be the book I had wanted to write. And it was. And of all my books, to this day it's the one of which I'm most proud.

Finally, it comes down to this: do you want to write the book? Would you write it, regardless? If the answer is yes, then welcome to the club. Have a seat. Get to work.

Exercises

1. I'm the editor of an online journal called *Defunct*, and we publish essays under two thousand words about everything that's had its day, from defunct technologies to defunct fads, music, political parties, you name it. The magazine doesn't trade in nostalgia so much as wit and insight into the past as well as the present. You can take a look at us at Defunctmag.com. Imagine that you're writing a proposal for *Defunct* (we don't actually accept proposals, but write one anyway). What defunct object or idea would you choose to write about and why? Why should we care? Your proposal shouldn't be more than two double-spaced pages.

2. While I was thinking about my latest editor's note for *Defunct*, I thought I might like to write about an unusual watch fob I own. I have a pocket watch collection, and the *fob* is the cord or chain tethered on one end to your clothing and on the other to your watch. One such fob I own dates from the Victorian era, and is made almost entirely of human hair. Gross, huh? If you saw this fob, you wouldn't believe it was made of hair. Half an inch thick and a foot long, it looks like some kind of rope, perhaps hemp, and is woven into an intricate pattern that alternates between a spiral shape and a more squared-off braid, and in three places it's held together by pentagon-shaped brass corsets. If you look closely, you'll notice individual hairs popping out, and then you'll most likely shiver in disgust. But hair art was common in the Victo-

rian era. Once I hit upon that, I typed "hair art" into my search engine and I soon ran across Leila's Hair Museum. Check it out (http://www .hairwork.com/leila/). Okay, did you imagine something as odd as this existed? Leila has been written about before, as it turns out, but no matter. Imagine you're going to write a piece about her. Start doing as much research as possible on hair art as an opener. Now imagine you were going to visit the hair museum (you must!) and interview Leila. What questions would you ask her? Now, write a two-page proposal in which you pitch to a magazine a piece (a hair piece) on Leila. Very important: what magazine would you pitch this to and why? Are you familiar with the magazine you're pitching? You had better be, or why bother?

3. Now do the same thing as above, but do it for real. Find a person with an unusual collection, hobby, or job and conduct as much research as you can on this person. Contact her and ask if you can do a series of interviews with her. Write a pitch before you've interviewed her. Then write another pitch after you've interviewed her. How has the focus of the pitch changed?

Conclusion

Say What You See

In the restaurant of the Presidente Hotel in Havana, Cuba, tourists from various countries mingle around the familiar breakfast buffet: meats and cheeses for the Europeans, a coffee machine for café latte, cappuccino, and espresso, a plate of guava, pineapple, and some kind of melon, a German guy sitting with a Havana Club T-shirt with the usual picture of Che emblazoned on it, a group of Russians by the pool to my left.

I'm here because I'm on a scouting trip for a workshop I'm going to be leading six months from now. Last week, I was in Poland attending the largest Jewish festival in the world, a festival founded by non-Jews twenty-three years ago. I'm working on a documentary about the festival with a young filmmaker. Next week, I'll be in Australia planning a nonfiction conference there.

Granted, my schedule is a little insane.

I suppose I'm the type of person who can't sit still, though I must have done so at some point or another to have written my books. The pull of the world is great on me, but I also love the solitude of writing. Sure, I had the requisite daiquiri at the Floridita Bar, where Hemingway used to hang out, but most nights I've stayed in and have simply written my impressions of what I've been seeing, trying to make sense of what I've experienced during the day. For me, writing is always a collaborative act, finally. While I have to do the heavy lifting, as it were, the people I meet are my collaborators, as are the books I read.

Xavier de Maistre and I are kindred spirits. As he wrote, "And why would [you] turn down the pleasures that are scattered along life's difficult path? They are so few and far between, so thin on the ground, that you'd need to be mad not to stop, and even turn away from your path, and pick up all of those that lie within your reach" (7). For me, the joy is in grabbing those opportunities.

In his book *Still Life with Oysters and Lemon* Mark Doty says it best, I think:

> We think that to find ourselves we need turn inward, examining the intricacies of origin, the shaping forces of personality. But "I" is just as much to be found in the world; looking outward, we experience the one who does the seeing. Say what you see and you experience yourself through your style of seeing and saying. (67)

In the introduction to this book, I tried to make the case for the value of the *I*. The rest of this book has tried to make a case for the value of the world outside of the *I*, or perhaps for a melding of the *I* and the world. It's not a matter of being self-indulgent. It's a matter of being honest, of writing reliably, and with humility. "Say what you see" is actually a rather bold command. Think of all the people throughout history who have been put to death for just that—for saying what they saw. Often, it's a matter of permission to become an authority or to bear witness, the notion that the individual with no credentials other than her individuality can see the world in a way that others might find value in.

Obviously, it's not easy. I think I've made that abundantly clear, but the rewards far outweigh the difficulties, I believe. To be a writer out in the world is to be a student of the world. While writing is nearly always a solitary act in which we necessarily come face to face with our deficiencies and our demons (and hopefully conquer them), the immersion writer makes the world part of his text. There are inherent narratives in anyone's life, and it's your job to discover and sometimes convey these narratives to the reader.

I recently learned that the Japanese word *sensei* doesn't mean "teacher" in the simple sense as I have long believed, but is better translated as "one who has gone before." It's in this spirit that I have written this book and used the examples I've threaded throughout—it helps to know that others have gone before. When I'm driving in a storm or at night and the visibility is low, I'm always grateful when up ahead I see a pair of taillights I can follow to keep me from drifting, to keep me on course to my destination, wherever that turns out to be.

For Further Reading

MEDIA MENTIONED IN THIS BOOK

IMMERSION MEMOIR

Agee, James, and Walker Evans. *Let Us Now Praise Famous Men*. New York: Houghton Mifflin Co., 2001.

Baker, Nicholson. *U and I: A True Story*. New York: Vintage, 1992.

Beavan, Colin. *No Impact Man: The Adventures of a Guilty Liberal Who Attempts to Save the Planet and the Discoveries He Makes about Himself and Our Way of Life in the Process*. New York: Farrar, Straus, and Giroux, 2009.

Bongiorno, Sarah. *A Year without "Made in China": One Family's True Life Adventure in the Global Economy*. New Jersey: Wiley, 2008.

Carlomagno, Mary. *Give It Up! My Year of Learning to Live Better with Less*. New York: William Morrow, 2005.

Carter, Hodding, IV. *Off the Deep End: The Probably Insane Idea that I Could Swim My Way through A Midlife Crisis—and Qualify for the Olympics*. Chapel Hill: Algonquin Books, 2008.

Chapman, Matthew. *Trials of the Monkey: An Accidental Memoir*. New York: Picador, 2001.

Cowser, Bob, Jr. *Dream Season: A Professor Joins America's Oldest Semi-Pro Football Team*. New York: Grove Press, 2005.

———. *Green Fields: Crime, Punishment, and a Boyhood Between*. New Orleans: University of New Orleans Press, 2010.

Cushing, Frank. *My Adventures in Zuni*. Palo Alto: American West Publishing Company, 1970.

Dobson, Ed. *The Year of Living Like Jesus: My Journey of Discovering What Jesus Would Really Do*. Grand Rapids, Mich.: Zondervan, 2009.

Dyer, Geoff. *Out of Sheer Rage: Wrestling with D. H. Lawrence*. New York: North Point Press, 1998.

Hawes, Elizabeth. *Camus, A Romance*. New York: Grove Press, 2009.

Hemley, Robin. *Do-Over! In Which a Forty-Eight-Year-Old Father of Three Returns to Kindergarten, Summer Camp, the Prom, and Other Embarrassments*. New York: Little, Brown, and Company, 2009.

Jacobs, A. J. *The Guinea Pig Diaries: My Life as an Experiment.* New York: Simon and Schuster, 2009.

———. *The Know-It-All: One Man's Humble Quest to Become the Smartest Man in the World.* New York: Simon and Schuster, 2004.

———. *The Year of Living Biblically.* New York: Simon and Schuster, 2008.

Kamen, Paula. *All in My Head: An Epic Quest to Cure an Unrelenting, Totally Unreasonable, and Only Slightly Enlightening Headache.* Cambridge, Mass.: De Capo Press, 2006.

Kingsolver, Barbara. *Animal, Vegetable, Miracle: A Year of Food Life.* New York: Harper Perennial, 2008.

Levine, Judith. *Not Buying it: My Year without Shopping.* New York: Free Press, 2007.

Lisik, Beth. *Helping Me Help Myself: One Skeptic, Twelve Self-Help Programs, One Whirlwind Year of Improvement.* New York: HarperCollins, 2009.

McDonald, Sam. *The Urban Hermit: A Memoir.* New York: St. Martin's Press, 2008.

Nerz, Ryan. *Eat this Book: A Year of Gorging and Glory on the Competitive Eating Circuit.* New York: St. Martin's Griffin, 2006.

Okrant, Robyn. *Living Oprah: My One-Year Experiment to Walk the Walk of the Queen of Talk.* New York: Center Street, 2010.

Powell, Julie. *Julie and Julia: My Year of Cooking Dangerously.* New York: Back Bay Books, 2006.

Shea, Ammon. *Reading the OED: One Man, One Year, 21,730 Pages.* New York: Perigee, 2009.

Smith, Alisa, and J. B. MacKinnon. *Plenty: Eating Locally on the 100-Mile Diet.* New York: Three Rivers Press, 2007.

Vincent, Nora. *Voluntary Madness: My Year Lost and Found in the Loony Bin.* New York: Viking, 2008.

Wallace, Danny. *Yes Man.* New York: Gallery Books, 2006.

IMMERSION JOURNALISM

Buford, Bill. *Among the Thugs.* New York: Vintage, 1993.

Conover, Ted. *Newjack: Guarding Sing Sing.* New York: Vintage, 2001.

Ehrenreich, Barbara. *Nickel and Dimed: On (Not) Getting By in America.* New York: Henry Holt and Company, 2008.

Goodman, Martin. *In Search of the Divine Mother: The Mystery of Mother Meera: Encountering a Contemporary Mystic.* New York: HarperCollins, 2001.

Griffin, John Howard. *Black Like Me.* New York: New American Library, 2003.

Hamilton-Paterson, James. *America's Boy: A Century of United States Colonialism in the Philippines*. New York: Henry Holt and Company, 1999.

Hemley, Robin. *Invented Eden*. Lincoln, Neb.: Bison Books, 2007.

Horwitz, Tony. *Confederates in the Attic: Dispatches from the Unfinished Civil War*. New York: Vintage, 1999.

Mackall, Joe. *Plain Secrets: An Outsider among the Amish*. New York: Beacon Books, 2008.

Maharidge, Dale, and Michael Williamson. *And Their Children After Them*. New York: Seven Stories Press, 2008.

Morris, Edmond. *Dutch: A Memoir of Ronald Reagan*. New York: Modern Library, 2000.

Orlean, Susan. *The Orchid Thief: A True Story of Beauty and Obsession*. New York: Ballantine, 2000.

Plimpton, George. *Out of My League: The Classic Hilarious Account of an Amateur's Ordeal in Professional Baseball*. Guilford, Conn.: Lyons Press, 2010.

————. *Paper Lion*. Guilford, Conn.: Lyons Press, 2009.

Roose, Kevin. *The Unlikely Disciple: A Sinner's Semester at America's Holiest University*. New York: Grand Central Publishing, 2009.

Shields, David. *Black Planet: Facing Race During an NBA Season*. Lincoln, Neb.: Bison Books, 2006.

Skloot, Rebecca. *The Immortal Life of Henrietta Lacks*. New York: Crown Books, 2010.

Vincent, Norah. *Self-Made Man: One Woman's Journey into Manhood and Back*. New York: Penguin, 2006.

Weiss, Philip. *American Taboo: A Murder in the Peace Corps*. New York: HarperCollins, 2004.

TRAVEL WRITING

Bissell, Tom. *The Father of All Things: A Marine, His Son, and the Legacy of Vietnam*. New York: Pantheon Books, 2007.

Burton, Richard F. *Personal Narrative of a Pilgrimage to Al-Madinah and Meccah, by Captain Sir Richard F. Burton, Edited by His Wife, Isabel Burton*, vol. 2. New York: Dover, 1964.

Cortazar, Julio, and Carol Dunlop. *Autonauts of the Cosmoroute, A Timeless Voyage from Paris to Marseilles*. Brooklyn: Archipelago Books, 2007.

de Botton, Alain. *Heathrow Diary*. New York: New Directions Publishing, 1994.

de Maistre, Xavier. *A Journey around My Room*. Trans. Andrew Brown. London: Hesperus Classics, 2004.

Francia, Luis H. *Eye of the Fish: A Personal Archipelago*. New York: Kaya Press, 2001.

Griest, Stephanie Elizondo. *Around the Bloc: My Life in Moscow, Beijing, and Havana*. New York: Villard: 2004.

———. *Mexican Enough: My Life between the Borderlines*. New York: Washington Square Press, 2008.

Griswold, Eliza. *The Tenth Parallel: Dispatches from the Fault Line between Christianity and Islam*. New York: Picador, 2011.

Gutkind, Lee. *Truckin' with Sam: A Father and Son, the Mick and the Dyl, Rockin' and Rollin', on the Road*. New York: State University of New York Press, 2010.

Hamilton-Paterson, James. *Playing with Water: Passion and Solitude on a Philippine Island*. London: MacMillan, 1987.

Heat-Moon, William Least. *Riverhorse: Across America by Boat*. New York: Penguin, 2001.

Herodotus. *The Histories*. Trans. Robin Waterfield. New York: Oxford University Press, 2008.

Heyerdahl, Thor. *Kon-Tiki: Across the Pacific in a Raft*. Mattituck, N.Y.: Amereon Ltd., 1993.

Hohn, Donovan. *Moby Duck: The True Story of 28,800 Bath Toys Lost at Sea and of the Beachcombers, Environmentalists, and Fools, Including the Author, Who Went in Search of Them*. New York: Viking, 2011.

Kohnstomm, Thomas. *Do Travel Writers Go to Hell? A Swashbuckling Tale of High Adventures, Questionable Ethics, and Professional Hedonism*. New York: Broadway Books, 2008.

Maniaty, Tony. *Shooting Balibo: Blood and Memory in East Timor*. Camberwell, Victoria, Australia: Viking Penguin Group, 2009.

Moore, Dinty. *The Accidental Buddhist: Mindfulness, Enlightenment, and Sitting Still, American-Style*. New York: Broadway Books, 1997.

Morris, Jan. *Trieste and the Meaning of Nowhere*. Cambridge, Mass.: Da Capo Press, 2002.

Paterniti, Michael. *Driving Mr. Albert: A Trip across America with Einstein's Brain*. New York: Dial Press, 2001.

Theroux, Paul. *Ghost Train to the Eastern Star: On the Tracks of the Great Railway Bazaar*. New York: Mariner Books, 2009.

———. *The Great Railway Bazaar: By Train through Asia*. Boston: Houghton Mifflin, 2006.

Vowell, Sarah. *Assassination Vacation*. New York: Simon and Schuster, 2006.

Weiner, Eric. *The Geography of Bliss: One Grump's Search for the Happiest Places in the World*. New York: Twelve, 2009.

OTHER NONFICTION

Benjamin, Walter. *Berlin Childhood around 1900*. Boston: Belknap Press, 2006.

Bernstein, Jane. *Bereft: A Sister's Story*. New York: North Point Press, 2000.

Daum, Meghan. *My Misspent Youth: Essays*. New York: Grove Press, 2001.

Doty, Mark. *Still Life with Oysters and Lemon: On Objects and Intimacy*. New York: Beacon Press, 2002.

Gardner, John. *The Art of Fiction*. New York: Vintage Books, 1991.

Hemley, Robin. *Turning Life into Fiction*. Saint Paul, Minn.: Graywolf Press, 2006.

Krakauer, Jon. *Into the Wild*. New York: Anchor Books, 2007.

Malcolm, Janet. *The Journalist and the Murderer*. New York: Vintage, 1990.

Pollan, Michael. *Omnivore's Dilemma: A Natural History of Four Meals*. New York: Penguin, 2007.

Rokeach, Milton. *The Three Christs of Ypsilanti*. New York: The New York Review of Books Classics, 2011.

Saunders, George. *The Braindead Megaphone*. New York: Riverhead Books, 2007.

Stone Sunstein, Bonnie, and Elizabeth Chiseri-Strater. *FieldWorking: Reading and Writing Research*, 4th ed. New York: St. Martin's Press, 2012.

OTHER MEDIA

de Maximy, Antoine, director. *J'irai Dormir a Hollywood*, 2008.

McElwee, Ross, director. *Sherman's March*, 1986.

Snyder, Rachel Louise, producer and host. *The Global Guru* (http://www.prx.org/series/31539-global-guru-radio).

CPSIA information can be obtained at www.ICGtesting.com
Printed in the USA
LVOW102112071112

306386LV00001B/3/P

9 780820 338507